ALSO BY JEANNE SAFER

Condom: And Other Essays on Love Lost and Found

cy: Liberating Siblings from a Lifetime of Rage, Shame, Secrecy, and Regret

enefits: How Losing a Parent Can Change an Adult's Life—for the Better

One: Life with a Difficult or Damaged Sibling

d Not Forgiving: A New Approach to Resolving Intimate Betrayal

otherhood: Choosing a Life Without Children

I L... You

bu...

You...

I Love You,

but I Hate

Your Politics

How to Protect Your
Intimate Relationships in a
Poisonous Partisan World

Jeanne Safer, Ph.D.

ALL
POINTS
BOOKS

The names and identifying characteristics of some persons described
in this book have been changed.

www.allpointsbooks.com

Library of Congress Cataloging-in-Publication Data

Names: Safer, Jeanne, author.
Title: I love you but I hate your politics : how to protect your intimate
  relationships in a poisonous partisan world / Jeanne Safer, PhD.
Description: First edition. | New York : All Points Books, 2019. | Includes
  bibliographical references and index.
Identifiers: LCCN 2019008430| ISBN 9781250200396 (hardcover) |
  ISBN 9781250200402 (ebook)
Subjects: LCSH: Political culture—United States. | Partisanship. |
  Interpersonal conflict. | Interpersonal relations—Political aspects. |
  Party affiliation—Social aspects.
Classification: LCC JK1726 .S24 2019 | DDC 158.2/4—dc23
LC record available at https://lccn.loc.gov/2019008430

Our books may be purchased in bulk for promotional, educational,
or business use. Please contact your local bookseller or the Macmillan
Corporate and Premium Sales Department at 1-800-221-7945, extension
5442, or by email at MacmillanSpecialMarkets@macmillan.com.

First Edition: June 2019

10 9 8 7 6 5 4 3 2 1

For my beloved friends, Bert and Nina Smiley

We love the things we love for what they are.

—Robert Frost, "Hyla Brook"

CONTENTS

I Love You,

but I Hate

Your Politics

INTRODUCTION

A House Divided

Intimate relationships in America are in crisis as never before, and political feuds are the reason.

A *Wall Street Journal*/NBC News postelection poll reported that close to one in three Americans had had a "heated argument" with a friend or family member who voted for the "other side"—the kind of arguments that fester.

Family gatherings have become minefields. A recent Quinnipiac poll showed that over two-thirds of respondents, ages eighteen to sixty-five-plus, were dreading political disputes on holidays.

An article in *Science* revealed that families with political conflicts are cutting their Thanksgiving meal short by up to an hour to avoid blow-ups around the turkey; they know no other way to prevent ugly confrontations.

In November 2018, *The New York Times* ran an article

on "safe topics to discuss this holiday season," and *Huffington Post* offered "17 Thanksgiving Conversation Topics That Aren't About Politics." Evidently we can't think of any on our own.

Unfriending on social media, the ultimate dis, has reached epidemic proportions. Pew Research polls reported that 27 percent of respondents had blocked or unfriended someone just before the 2016 election. Those numbers continue to escalate ominously; erasing a relationship has become an acceptable way to disagree.

Gone are the days when couples could simply avoid areas of conflict over public policy, as my own parents did (my father was an Eisenhower Republican and my mother a liberal Democrat); I never heard them discuss, much less quarrel about, politics. But in the sixties, the era of Vietnam, politics invaded every crevice of private life. The Bush era, the Iraq War, and fights over Supreme Court nominees escalated the right/left conflict, and dialogue across the aisle became rarer and rarer. Now, in the Trump era, it has disappeared entirely: the political has become the personal, making lovers and friends with different party affiliations a vanishing breed.

A major culprit, an ominous new wrinkle in the current crisis, is the partisan media, including the degraded state of discourse on cable and talk radio, the twenty-four-hour news cycle, and, above all, the explosion of social media that has invaded every nook and cranny of our craniums. Like children imitating their parents, people mimic what they see and hear onscreen and online, to the detriment of any kind of dialogue. They have become so unused to actual conversation with the other side that they can only deliver partisan diatribes. "You voted for that *monster!*" was the opening conversational gambit of a progressive woman interview subject of mine at a romantic dinner her conservative boyfriend had made for her. She was mimicking her friends and her news sources.

Online hostility gives people a spurious sense of power over those they cannot convince. Several people I interviewed had actually been unfriended on social media by their own parents, ended romances (in one case, broke an engagement), or unfriended their siblings or erstwhile close companions in reaction to online content they deemed offensive. They never even tried to work it out. Such a reaction to differences of opinion is insane but has become disturbingly normalized, and almost automatic. One-half of my interview subjects reported unfriending or being unfriended over politics—and only one of them re-friended the person and apologized to him. Broken bonds are tough to repair, and it may not be possible to re-friend someone even if you have regrets or second thoughts.

The impact of this poisonous political climate on our bonds with spouses, lovers, family, and friends—abetted by the ranting 24/7 news outlets—is disastrous and tragic, and it is continuing to escalate with no end in sight. Our social circles have become so insulated and homogeneous that many people, particularly younger people, rarely venture outside the group of the like-minded and have virtually no voluntary contact with anyone with whom they disagree. No wonder we demonize the opposition.

Researchers from Stanford University reported that intermarriage across party lines had plummeted to just 9 percent from 20 percent in the late twentieth century. No wonder so many mixed-political couples feel isolated; they have so few peers, and their friends cannot relate to them.

An article in *The Journal of Politics* in 2011 reported that parents worry more about their children marrying across party lines than across racial or religious ones, and that political compatibility has replaced even physical attractiveness as the fundamental quality to seek in a potential mate.

Politics is also tearing established couples apart. According to Wakefield Research, one in ten couples is ending their relationship because of battles over politics—a phenomenon that has been labeled "the Trump divorce." For younger millennials, the appalling statistic is 22 percent.

And there is no more dangerous indicator of how serious a threat political conflicts are to love and civility than this: Wakefield Research found that 20 percent of couples are now fighting more ferociously and frequently over Trump's policies than about money, the most contentious marital issue of all time.

Even psychotherapy, the last bastion of the personal, has

become politicized; in over four decades in practice, I've never seen anything like it. A patient of mine seriously considered terminating our long and fruitful relationship because I questioned his desperate plan to move to Canada after Trump won the election; we worked it out, and he decided to stay put, but the intensity of his outrage and sense of betrayal at my failure to applaud his scheme—which was related to his dealings with his unsupportive, pro-Trump parents—was disconcerting.

These irreparable rifts are part of virtually everyone's experience, and the list of casualties keeps growing.

⚜

As a psychoanalyst and relationship specialist in practice for forty-five years, and a liberal Democrat married for thirty-nine years to a senior editor at *National Review,* the leading conservative journal of opinion, I've been writing about navigating this divide in my own life for decades. My husband and I have also written about it together and have appeared jointly in the media to discuss our surprising relationship. People are often astonished that the two of us have managed to accomplish a feat that many believe is impossible.

I also host a podcast entitled "I Love You, but I HATE Your Politics" on which I speak to a fascinating array of mixed-political couples of all sorts, so others in this situation can feel that they have peers.

Since the 2016 presidential election, I have become the go-to expert on how to make a mixed-political relationship flourish. Readers and listeners have deluged me with desperate requests for advice on how to have a political disagreement with an intimate partner without mutually assured destruction. Their predicaments run the gamut from touching and amusing to almost unbearably painful. Among the people who contacted me: a man attached both to his comic decal of Trump urinating on Hillary Clinton and to his liberal girlfriend who demanded he remove it from his windshield; a liberal son who feared that his conservative father would physically attack him because of their political differences; a conservative brother who worried that his uncontrollable political rants were destroying his relationship with his beloved left-leaning sister, the only relative who had yet to unfriend him.

I Love You, but I Hate Your Politics is my response to their pleas. My goal in writing this book is to analyze the psychology of compulsive political fighting and to counsel people on how to extricate themselves from it. My analysis and recommendations are based on fifty interviews with individuals and couples who are trying to find their way out of constant political bickering with those they love. Some of the people I talk to, and whom you will meet in these pages, are still struggling to understand these bruising battles; and others, who have succeeded in transforming their fights, share the secrets to their success.

Everyone I spoke to felt relieved and encouraged by our conversation, even people I never expected to respond. It is to them that I owe many of the insights and the life-changing advice you will find here.

Couples of all kinds feel increasingly desperate about this problem, which seems to be getting worse by the minute and from which almost nobody is exempt. A seventy-nine-year-old retired general told me that his closest friend of sixty years stopped talking to him when he voted for Trump, a loss that still devastates him but he feels he cannot repair. There is a serious crisis in civility in private as well as public life. *I Love You, but I Hate Your Politics* shows you how to put a stop to it, in your own heart and with those who matter most to you.

Young people, who have very few models of civility or tolerance in the political realm to draw on, and are hermetically encased in partisan media and internet bubbles, are especially at risk. Recent research by Match.com shows that 47 percent of millennials would not even consider dating someone with different political beliefs. There is now a foolproof way for them (and their elders) to date only people who agree with them politically. On RedStateDate/BlueStateDate the poster children for these twin sites were the Reagans and the Obamas looking into each other's eyes—"True Love Exists!" the captions said—and you could find your "politically correct" match using their "uniquely progressive match system" and "Meet Republican Singles in Under 2 minutes!" For the ultra-niche markets, there are Trump-Singles and BernieSingles, as well as proliferating sites for progressives, libertarians, and other political sects.

These sites set people up to be disappointed, because political affinity alone is virtually worthless as a reflection of genuine like-mindedness or good character and probably ranks alongside sharing an astrological sign as a predictor of lasting compatibility. Unfortunately, guaranteed political compatibility guarantees no other kind. Nor is it a litmus test for moral rectitude.

Luckily for me, no such tool existed when I met and married my politically incorrect husband (whom I met in a singing group) in 1980. Otherwise I never would have discovered that it is possible to have everything in common with someone except politics. I tell the story of our most contentious issue and how our responses to it evolved in the last chapter of this book.

⁜

There is no dearth of advice on how to navigate the new world of interpersonal conflict that our contentious partisan environment has created. It ranges from the preposterous—a headline in *Harper's Bazaar* helpfully recommended, "If Your Husband Voted for Trump, Just Divorce Him!"—to serious works on the moral assumptions underlying political opinions, techniques to manage ideological disagreements by preventing or diverting angry interactions, and general conflict resolution strategies that could be applied to any fight. But the advice even the best of these counselors offer, though often sensible or enlightening, is of limited efficacy. Many of the people who urgently contacted me for advice had read extensively in their search for help but did not find the practical assistance they sought to enable them to change their charged interactions with the other side, or an understanding of how they got embroiled in endless tormenting fights in the first place. What they found explained the "what" but not the "why." They sought me out because other sources had failed.

The available advice falls into several categories, all of which miss the main reason political fights are so disturbing and recalcitrant.

One approach in the most popular books people turn to for help with this problem is to present a moral typology so the reader can identify his or her own approach to politics and realize how subjective are the attitudes and opinions that grow out of it, and why alternative stances are so infuriating.

A subject of mine told me how enlightening it was for her to read a description of her moral type that explained why she felt driven to convert her Trump-supporting mother-in-law to her own progressive views. However, this information did not stop her from continuing to badger a woman with whom she had an otherwise excellent relationship; nor did it cause her to question why she persisted against the wishes and admonitions of everyone she knew.

Another type of book offers strategies for resolving conflicts in general—good to know, but not specifically tailored to the current explosion of political venom. A third genre advises readers how to frame a political discussion in ways that defuse animosity, without analyzing what motivates the combatants to persevere in the first place.

It may be illuminating and comforting to identify your ethical attitude, learn conflict resolution techniques, or seek tips to turn down the temperature once a fight has started, but none of these strategies will help you understand the emotional origins of the dispute or reveal why you keep trying desperately to win fights that are unwinnable. I offer something radically different from any of these: an in-depth analysis of the underlying psychological motivation behind political battles.

It is often suggested that people list their "triggers," the political topics that provoke them the most. Some may find it helpful to identify what their hot-button issues are—although most of us (and all of my subjects) know them already, as I certainly do. Knowing what sets you off does little to prevent you from getting sucked into a dispute. Only understanding why you rise to the bait—or dangle it yourself—will help you stop.

There is an effective way out of the emotional crisis we are in. But we have been looking for help in all the wrong places. Psychology, not politics, is the key to understanding and changing the compulsive battles that are tearing us apart.

I believe that ongoing political conflict in intimate relationships is what psychoanalysts call the "manifest content"—the superficial expression—of much more profound, or "latent," underlying conflicts. Our fights are rarely about the overt issues that spark them, particularly when they are repetitive and emotionally devastating.

Endless arguments between couples who love each other ultimately stem from grandiose fantasies about the power we have over others, and from our compulsion to exercise that power to change their minds and make them a reflection of ourselves. The interviews and analysis I provide—and the changes in heart and mind that arise from them—leave no doubt that this is true, and I explain what motivates us so compulsively in my chapter on Relentless Hope.

Even though I preach tolerance and empathy across the aisle, there are exceptions that must be acknowledged and honored. Every one of us has nonnegotiable limits to our ability to accept alternative points of view with which we passionately disagree; you won't find encouragement to tolerate a mate or a friend or family member who is a recalcitrant racist, a sexist, or a supporter of the antifa or the alt-right. One of my interview subjects reveals how she came to reject such a person (he also had his charms, which made her hesitate). Only then did she realize that his re-pugnant opinions were fundamental to his character in a way she had not noticed when she was in love with him. Sometimes politics, particularly extreme politics, is an in-extricable and pernicious part of a person's character. This book will help you identify the difference between legiti-mate and dangerous alternative viewpoints.

People become demoralized and feel hopeless when they do not get the help they ardently seek and need, which is why books dispensing superficial advice proliferate but do not satisfy. To seek help for a crisis in your relationship but to receive instead recommendations that provide a mere Band-Aid and little direction on how to think deeply about the problem leads people to conclude that there is no way out. Then they blame themselves, the other person, or their ideological differences for the problem. Political fights are so compelling that it's easy to be swept up in the turbulent surface and become irrational. But authentic change in how we can relate to others only comes when we comprehend our own feelings and their origins. This is why making lists of issues, identifying cognitive styles, or applying behavioral strategies without insight will make no lasting difference in how you act or react in a political fight. Change comes from understanding alone.

No other book offers the unique and effective blueprint for insight and change that you'll find here—an analysis not of the content of your fights, or how to turn them to your advantage, but of how to grasp their underlying psychological origin and meaning for *you*. The key to insight is to recognize that you are the problem (not your right- or left-wing adversary), as well as the potential solution. This is actually good news, because changing yourself is possible, while changing others is not.

The key to lasting change, I believe, is realizing that political fights in intimate relationships **are not really about politics.** They stem from our compulsion to change other people's minds so that they will feel and think as we do. Even if they do not and cannot, we keep desperately trying to transform them. This is the counterintuitive thesis of my book, and the key to the effectiveness of its recommendations. If politics alone were the source of discord, people who disagreed would never be able to have a civil serious discussion—something many couples have learned to do: my subjects did, my husband and I did, and so can you.

I bring a unique set of professional and personal qualifications to the role of adviser to the politically desperate. My own marriage is living proof that two people of goodwill but diametrically opposed politics can not only survive but thrive, even in the current malignly polarized environment. My husband and I have learned through experience how to deal with our differences and protect our love; you can read about how we did it in chapter 9.

I have created a unique therapeutic method tailored

specifically to the needs of couples, friends, and family members battling over politics, which individuals can also use when dealing with recalcitrant opponents. It's based on behavioral interventions and psychological interpretations. What I do with couples is different from traditional couples therapy, because I focus exclusively on a particular type of noxious interaction with deep emotional roots and offer techniques to achieve insight and change on your own, alone and together. Understanding what's really going on and why in these terrible fights opens your eyes and gives you options you could not imagine before. You will see many examples of this happening in the interviews in this book.

I am not a referee; nor am I a couples counselor, a debate coach, or a mediator. My job is to identify and to help individuals and couples recognize the psychological meaning of their fights and to explore their emotional basis. I help both combatants identify their emotional contributions to the problem, and I suggest changes based on my understanding of the psychological origins of the dispute and its meaning to each participant. I am not a fight coach but an empathic observer and analyst of emotions and how they compel us. People find this new approach revelatory, relieving, and life changing.

In the last chapter, you'll find "The Politics Doctor's Ten Proven Ways to Stop a Political Fight Before It Starts," a compendium of recommendations gleaned from my own marriage, my decades of professional experience, and the personal experience of my interview subjects who have succeeded in improving their relationships by applying these principles to their political discussions. These and the other practical suggestions I offer can be applied to any fraught relationship. You will learn how to convert potentially acrid exchanges into actual conversations instead of bickering and bitterness—a tall order in the current climate, to be sure, but it can be done.

We will never entirely eliminate all the distress, anger, and anxiety that serious political conflicts create, but we can stop endangering our most important relationships. In the words of Proverbs, "A soft answer turneth away wrath: but grievous words stir up anger."

Learning to do this takes work, and it's worth it.

※

We have a comforting fantasy that those who agree with our politics are like-minded in the ways that matter most. This is not necessarily true, and it idealizes our own opinions while demonizing the other side. I believe that neither political party has a lock on the truth, decency, or humanity. Or on selfishness, fanaticism, arrogance, or rigidity. You will find many vivid examples of each in these pages. In my chapter "What Is a Core Value?" I advocate nothing less than a reevaluation of our authentic moral foundations.

The fight to preserve intimacy in a divided world is the only fight worth having. Couples must volunteer as allies on the same side.

You are about to meet a cross-section of Americans who are honestly, and movingly, struggling to accomplish the difficult but rewarding feat—a feat many people believe is hopeless even to attempt—of transforming their political discourse through insight, empathy, self-knowledge, and sensitivity to their partners. It can be done! Not one of them wants to go back to their old ways of fighting—the raised voices, the slammed doors, and the lack of good-night kisses.

I promise you won't either.

1

The Endless Fight

How to Lose a Political Battle, Every Time

Many of the people you will meet in these pages are embroiled in fights with their nearest and dearest that they never can win. In other aspects of their lives they are considerate, caring, and intelligent, but when their political hackles are raised they become obsessed, unreachable—even unhinged. Often one partner attacks the other, who is trying to keep the peace or avoid the onslaught, and the dispute becomes less about a particular ideological position than about the unbearable fact that an immutable, fundamental difference exists between two people who love each other.

Below are some surefire techniques for guaranteeing the worst possible outcome to such a confrontation, all of which the intimate political combatants I spoke with and describe in this chapter and the next have actually employed. Do *not* imagine that any one of them will work any better for you than it did for them. You will not succeed where they failed. Do not try these at home!

- Thrust unsolicited partisan articles into your spouse's hands at the breakfast table, or deliver them daily to his or her in-box. Then conduct an interrogation about the contents, which will certainly convince the other person to embrace your point of view.

- Email a PowerPoint presentation entitled "Re-education" to your best friend, who supports neither side. This will show her the error of her ways and earn you her gratitude for helping her see the light.

- If your boyfriend makes what you consider a racially insensitive comment, give him a lecture on the history of slavery in America. Shove him into his seat to make sure he pays attention.

- If a minor difference of opinion in a political spat—so trivial that the two of you still vote for the same candidate—enrages your partner so much that he breaks your marble table, follow him out of the room and smash his cell phone into smithereens in revenge. This is most persuasive when each of you has had at least one drink.

Passionate political disputes can wreak havoc with even the best marriages and other committed relationships. Couples who have lived together harmoniously for decades, and who agree on practically everything else—including those who voted for different candidates in past elections—suddenly feel threatened to the core as never before, as though some awful truth about their mate that irreparably violates their trust has been exposed. They feel stuck in an interminable battle to change the other person's mind, a campaign that has no beginning, no end, and from which they cannot extricate themselves. Most of the time they can't even remember what they were fighting about the day before, because it's always, numbingly, the same. These days, political infidelity evokes emotions just as intense and devastating as the old-fashioned kind used to do.

The Liberal Turncoat

Sandy Kaplan, a sixty-seven-year-old lifelong liberal who had a long career as a federal law enforcement officer, still cannot accept that Dan, her husband of twenty-nine years, voted for Trump instead of Hillary in 2016. Until then he had always been as progressive as she—and a sincere feminist ("I think it's time for a woman president," he'd said more than once, and meant it)—but some successful business dealings he'd had with Trump convinced him that "Trump gets things done," and he became a fervent supporter of the Republican candidate.

"It was unbearable—I couldn't respect his position. We'd always had the same politics. When I found out how he voted I wanted to kill him—and I had the means," she said, only half-jokingly referring to the fact that she packed heat professionally.

Suddenly there was "nothing we agreed on," as though this one vote of his canceled out everything else they still had in common; for her, being out of sync politically seemed to undermine what she admired about his character. Even though she appreciated his pride when she provided security for the Women's March in Washington ("I admire everything she does," he told me), she couldn't forgive him.

Sandy tirelessly, combatively labored to change Dan's mind back, despite his total stonewalling of her efforts and the serious escalation of tension between them that ensued. Eventually they decided to avoid the topic. "But," she admitted, "I violated the agreement." So shocked, desperate, and outraged was she that she almost lost her formidable sense of humor.

The bruising fights continued long after the election, each one instigated by her. "I finally said we shouldn't have any more political discussions at all," she said, "but he adhered and I didn't." Why didn't she take her own advice? "I feel vindocated every time Trump commits some new outrage, and I always point it out to him. It's the only time I feel good."

For a momentary gratification, Sandy risks endangering the bond that sustains her, the bulwark of her life. She is violating one of the prime directives for mixed-political couples: *no gloating*. It never changes anybody's opinions, but it's a foolproof alienator. She fans the flames every time she sticks it to him, which is basically daily; a more volatile or combative husband would never tolerate her provocations or would retaliate. This is a situation where, because of their temperamental differences, rational, mutual political discussion cannot happen. She desperately needs another outlet for her wrath if she wants to do her part to preserve this otherwise excellent marriage.

In Sandy's mind, even Dan's spotless feminist credentials are now suspect, forever besmirched by his enthusiasm for a man she abhors, although the reason for his vote—as was the case for many people—came from convictions about policy, not character. This was too much cognitive dissonance for her to tolerate. It was impossible for her to accept that her husband's personal work experience with his candidate had changed something, but certainly not *everything*.

The disillusionment was totally one-sided; Dan makes no attempt to force his ideas down his wife's throat and feels it's fine for her to vote and to think as she pleases. Only she cannot bear the change.

Sandy had come up with a novel method of coping with her profound disillusionment: she convinced herself that she had actually succeeded in changing Dan's mind back to being in lockstep with hers. She based this on the fact that he stopped contradicting her and avoided political "discussions"—harangues by her—assiduously. She only found out that he hadn't budged an iota when he told her about his interview with me. To her credit, she found this amusing and felt abashed.

Sandy has noticed that Dan "doesn't defend Trump anymore," but she hasn't figured out that he's doing it tactically to keep the peace, not because he's had a change of heart. She still cuts articles out of the paper and thrusts them across the breakfast table. "Every morning, I'm criticized," he said with resignation. "What do you do when she hands you an article?" I wondered. "Nothing," he said. "I draw a blank, because then there's no argument—I've found that if you don't say anything back, mostly she drops it." Ultimately, it is his more placid, forgiving, avoidant temperament that keeps the peace between them.

No Fox News for You

Frequently something much deeper than politics threatens a marriage, although it is expressed in political terms. Ideological disagreement obsesses couples and blinds them to the underlying dynamics that drive them apart. These fights can be symptomatic—indicators of underlying fault lines that were masked by political agreement earlier on. The combatants cannot see what's really going on, which is often carried by the tone, as much as the content, of their exchanges, and they remain embroiled in the surface issues rather than recognizing and addressing the underlying emotions, so nothing can be resolved.

Mark and Phyllis Halperin, a long-married couple in their midsixties, were so distressed by the perpetual political tension that was damaging their relationship that they interrupted a holiday vacation in Manhattan to come and talk to me about it.

Mark was tenderly solicitous of his disconsolate wife, who was near tears of sorrow mingled with bitter outrage throughout our conversation. He sat close to her, kept his hand on her shoulder, spoke to her soothingly, and did not rise to the bait she amply provided. Clearly, theirs was a perpetual fight (and overtly a one-sided one), and this was only a single day's episode.

The tension between the Halperins had been building

since he switched party allegiances in the George W. Bush years, but it boiled over when he voted for Trump.

She has neither accepted nor forgiven his apostasy and believes it destroyed their shared world. "We've moved apart in our basic values," she says. "I can only recoil." Like Dan Kaplan, Mark keeps his political opinions to himself ("I mostly button my lip or occasionally make a meek argument," he says) and never disputes Phyllis's right to disagree. In fact, he feels empathy for her views on social welfare policy, many of which he knows are based on her long experience in the field—in which they both have advanced professional degrees—even though he has not shared them for years. To his mind, their different views do no damage to their intimacy. "Let's concentrate on everything else we still have in common," he says. This would be excellent advice if she could only take it. He is sincerely disturbed that she feels so threatened by his change of allegiance, and feels as rejected as she does. They are both suffering, and both stuck.

Mostly she talked and he listened, interspersed with sympathetic glances and gentle words of self-defense. There was an underlying sense of hopelessness and desperation in both of them, as though they were embroiled in a battle with no possible resolution. I felt I was witnessing an oft-repeated ritual that went nowhere, in which it was nearly impossible to intervene.

Phyllis considers the fact that he turned right while she

stayed left a personal betrayal of everything she holds dear; it has destroyed her equilibrium. How could he really love her if he did this to her? Not only has he rejected her philosophy, but he has abandoned her altogether and left her completely alone. "You're my social network," she says with real distress. She feels she has lost him utterly because they no longer agree on everything, ignoring (as is also the case with the Kaplans) large expanses of common ground; for example, Mark agreed to make Phyllis's sister, a committed Communist, the guardian for their disabled daughter—hardly a decision based on ideology. Phyllis is deaf to her and Mark's similarities and the fundamental strength of their relationship because she focuses entirely on the one thing she has lost: lockstep political agreement. She takes this literally as the problem, when it is only a symptom.

The most striking example of Phyllis's tyranny (and her way of punishing her "unfaithful" spouse) is her censoring of his access to the free press. "I forbid him Fox News," she says unapologetically. He is not permitted to watch the channel, which is her nemesis, even in the basement of their three-story house:

"I can't stand to know you're down there with it on, watching something I abhor."

"But I'm mostly taping, and I only listen to a little bit of what I tape."

"No you don't, and besides it doesn't matter—you tape everything."

For Phyllis, those tapes, whether he listens to them or not, are radioactive, pulsing up from the basement three floors down and spewing poisonous political vapors that contaminate the atmosphere.

To my dismay, I saw that Mark mostly went along with this prohibition (with some furtive forays into *Hannity*) and capitulated to her decree in order to keep the peace. When I said that it was unfair and would cause anyone to become resentful, she was unmoved; since she cannot change his mind, exiling and controlling him are her only options.

She's a sad tyrant, but a tyrant nonetheless, preventing her husband from being himself and having his own ideas because only hers are kosher in her eyes. Blind to the genuine love he showers her with, and which she also feels toward him outside of politics, she only felt secure when they had a total mind-meld. Now that he no longer provides it, she must be avenged.

The politically betrayed, regardless of gender or party affiliation, are rigid extremists who consider any significant difference of opinion apostasy. These people are so literal-minded and exacting that they cannot conceive that they could actually share, and continue to share, the most important basic values with someone with whom they disagree politically. This attitude gives politics far too central a role and causes people to focus on beliefs rather than actions.

Why does Phyllis equate political unanimity with true love? Her history provides the answer: she came from a left-wing family, and her parents marched on protests together. This is her image of an ideal marriage, and she needs to replicate that literal like-mindedness—as though joint marchers could have no fundamental disagreements, as every couple must. She sees Mark's political shift as a betrayal and a rejection of her when, in fact, it harkens back to his own past. He is, he told me, re-identifying with the conservative father he once repudiated but with whom he made peace and now shares a worldview. People can change their minds as they grow older for all sorts of reasons, and rarely is it in reaction to their mate, or any reflection on their marriage. In fact, political unanimity can actually mask underlying problems in a relationship, which emerge with a vengeance when a couple's politics diverge.

Why does Mark tolerate the way Phyllis punishes him? He is as afraid of losing her as she is of having lost him. His passivity empowers her aggression, and he is too afraid of her fragility to confront the damage she is doing to what is essentially a close, loving, long-enduring, and mutual bond. Neither of them realizes that their marriage has shown itself to be strong enough to endure despite differences of opinion.

A glimmer of hope occurred at the very end of our conversation. I had mentioned by way of example that people often attempt to change a mate's mind by inundating the culprit with unsolicited partisan articles from their own point of view, a practice that is both provocative and ineffective. To my surprise, Phyllis admitted, "I do that." "I recommend that you stop immediately," I said. "It will improve things." Mark concurred: "I'd like to find a way for us both to emphasize all that we still have in common." "I can stop sending articles," she offered, and I was encouraged to hear it. If she also learns to tolerate him watching whatever news he wants—wherever he wants—they could have the beginnings of a real détente.

***

An extraordinary evolution—one I never expected—occurred for this couple as a result of our conversation. I wrote to Mark to ask how they were doing, because their distress had made a deep impression on me and I was worried about them. They seemed embroiled in an eternal battle with no possible winners. This is his reply:

> I think our conversation with you helped a lot. We've been having an easier time staying in the nonpolitical realm and finding mutual enjoyment there. For my wife, I think our chat gave her the sense that we are not so unusual and that was comforting. Your comment about knowing people with all the right politics who are still assholes (and, of course, the very good people with the "wrong" politics) was an important reminder.

> People can change.

How Can I Trust You Ever Again?

Men are just as susceptible as women to Spousal Political Conversion Anxiety Syndrome, a diagnosis I have discovered that has yet to make it into the *DSM-5* (the standard psychiatric diagnostic manual) but has already reached epidemic proportions. Even in an otherwise close relationship, either partner can be overcome with a sense of catastrophe and a loss of solidarity if the other shifts allegiances, even to the point of paranoia.

Turkish-born Mehmet Aksoy, a software designer, and his American wife, Anna, a yoga instructor, both in their midthirties, have been married four years and have two children. Mehmet was born in Istanbul—he was raised as a Muslim but has become an atheist—and emigrated to the United States with his parents. When the family became citizens, they all joined the Democratic Party, and in the 2016 election they were avid Clinton supporters.

Since they never discussed it, Mehmet assumed that Anna was in total political sync with him (which had never been entirely true; Sandy Kaplan made the same mistake about her husband, Dan). Then Anna horrified him by stating on Facebook that she had not voted for Obama and had officially become a Republican. She never told him this directly to his face, perhaps because she anticipated his reaction and wanted to avoid a confrontation—which, of course, had the opposite effect; knowing his sensitivity and its sources in his traumatic experience with his parents, it would have been a much better idea to let him know and take the consequences directly, rather than doing what he had to perceive as sneaking around. He was so upset that she wound up deleting her account to keep the peace. He still hasn't gotten over it, and he made her so miserable about her new affiliation that she contemplated leaving him, even though politics was their only acknowledged area of serious discord, the focus of potent unconscious anxieties for this otherwise loving and sensible man.

Things did not improve when she decided to wholeheartedly support Trump, even though she had not voted for him. This really made her the traitor in the bedroom.

"All of a sudden, he feels it's an extreme, fundamental issue," she told me. "He grew up in an environment in which Democrats are good and Republicans are evil." Although she has strong opinions about the issues of the day, she feels no need to impose them on her husband, or even to discuss their differences; to my surprise, this live-and-let-live attitude was considerably more common in people I talked to who were on the right than those who were on the left, perhaps because the left is currently out of power and its adherents feel more of a need to defend their position; this may change with the political tides. "I have my own point of view—it's not a problem for me," she says. "I don't need anyone to agree with me."

She puts politics in perspective. "When I'm lying on my deathbed, this stuff won't be a big thing for me."

However, Mehmet believes that Anna's opinions cannot really be her own but instead are a result of brainwashing by the right wing. Why? As Anna said, "Because he had a vision of being married to a wife who mirrors him on everything, so if we're not in complete agreement there's something wrong; he's the emotional one." He is threatened by a wife who thinks for herself, even though she clearly cares deeply about him. I pointed out to her that Mehmet's dictatorial insistence on like-mindedness, which he clings to in order to counteract his doubts and fears about her fidelity in general, actually pushes her away and alienates her in areas that have nothing to do with politics. "I never thought about it that way," she says. "But it's true that he believes I've changed much more radically than I actually have. I think his real fear is that if I can change my mind about politics, maybe I'll wake up one day and want a new husband, too—someone more in line with my current views."

Once again, personal history affects perception: this is what Mehmet's mother actually did, even though politics had nothing to do with her infidelity. Mehmet has never gotten over the trauma of his parents' vicious divorce and its impact on his childhood. He is unknowingly projecting his fears about all women, and his experience with one in particular, onto his wife. The situation is extremely stressful for her, but she knows that their relationship is solid in every other aspect and that his fears are really about his past, not his present. Eventually he will figure out that she has no plans to turn him in for a new Trump/Republican model. "A lot of self comes out in politics," Anna concludes, wisely.

Under the Rug

Politics is much too central for these contentious couples. At least one partner in each is obsessed with his or her own beliefs and consumed by efforts to impose them on the other person. Speaking your mind is not always the best policy and is often more of an outlet for aggression than a genuine attempt to communicate.

However, it is also possible to put a relationship in jeopardy by talking about political differences too little or not at all; suppressing, too, can take a toll on intimacy.

Phobic avoidance of any political discourse is not the same as a joint, judicious decision by two people who recognize and accept that they are too far apart in their views—or that their personalities are too combative—to be able to converse productively about them. This is a rational, and usually effective, way to navigate potentially inflammatory differences; we will meet people who have accomplished this later on. However, when anxiety and unacknowledged anger underlie the silence, trouble is always around the corner. A subliminal sense of discontent, anger, and uncertainty lurks beneath everyday life, ready to emerge and make trouble, even for couples who are otherwise made for each other.

※

Ted and Jen Schwartz certainly have no dearth of wit, although it deserts them when politics comes up. Several years into their fifteen-year marriage—he is fifty, she is forty-eight, and they have two sons—Jen, who was raised a Christian and is a passionate left-leaning Democrat, remarked, "Of all the Jews I had to fall in love with, I find the *one* Jew who's a Republican." To his credit, Ted thought this was hilarious and added a quip of his own: "My wife is a believer in the inherent Satanic leaning of members of the Republican Party." But even the briefest, seemingly benign foray into ideological waters is fraught for them.

Recently, in a local election, Ted said he "let her see my ballot before feeding it into the machine," and then attempted to explain why he had voted for the Independent candidate instead of the Democrat, which infuriated Jen. "The 'exchange of ideas' only lasted seven or eight minutes," he said, "but I was surprised that I was capable of causing her that much pain over a local vote." I was surprised that he would show her his ballot and, when he exercised his right to cast it for whoever he wished, that he accepted her outraged reaction as legitimate. Why did he have to go to such lengths to mollify her?

Ted, a committed anti-Trump libertarian, tries tirelessly to avoid controversy; he even subscribes to a variety of political journals from all across the spectrum—the only person I interviewed who does so. "The truth doesn't belong to one side only. I don't want to get trapped in one point of view, and this helps us not to fight," he explained. "By not being too rigid I can really listen."

But does he? Ted claims that his only attempt to sway his wife is to "continually urge her to listen to more news outlets than just NPR," although he is careful not to insist, let alone subject her to the right-wing media he prefers. The trickiest issue they face is how to discuss their disparate views with their sons. "I like to present many sides of an issue, whereas she usually tries not to 'confuse' them with all the nuances; this translates into 'Everything Trump does is always evil and there is no good to be found in anything that did, can, or will happen during his presidency'; I'm only 60 to 75 percent on board with that"—an implicit if jocular criticism of what he considers Jen's fanatic allegiance to the Democratic party line. Like Mark Halperin, he appreciates his wife's "really big, caring heart," although he is convinced that "throwing federal money around [as she advocates] makes no difference."

Ted bends over backward to be conciliatory, but his efforts do not really improve things between him and Jen, or lessen the incompatibility of their differences. His politics gets under her skin, and he doesn't take her views seriously; both are angrier than they think, and it shows more than they know.

When I spoke to Jen,[†] I got quite a different take on their interaction. Ted had presented himself to me as fair-minded to a fault, but his wife saw him as a "right-wing fanatic" who fled conflict even more desperately than she did. She also told me—although I saw no evidence of this—that she considered herself intellectually inadequate and ill informed compared to him and unable to refute his arguments, if they ever dared to have one. "He speaks so well," she said, "that I feel like I can't defend myself." For them, arguing itself is the problem, not political savvy.

As is usually the case, the way they deal with conflict is rooted in their pasts. "Politics was a landmine in both our childhoods," Jen told me. Her parents went to great lengths to avoid political confrontations, while Ted's had such bruising ones that he vowed never to repeat the experience and to protect his children from them. The result, in Jen's picturesque phrase, is that in their home, "things are under-rug slapped."

[†] Depending on a couple's preference, I interviewed them together or separately. In some cases, only one of them was willing to talk about the conflict.

"There was a lot of yelling in my home, which I hated," said Ted. "I don't want to fight with the person I love—that's why I make it my value to always try to get a bunch of different perspectives on things." Jen, however, freely admits that she "reads only Trump-bashing news" and has no interest in expanding her ideological horizons.

Ted's ploy was so successful that Jen "didn't even realize that we didn't agree" in the first years of their marriage, but when the awful truth came out, she told me, "I felt lonely because I care about these things so much; he's the rock in our relationship, and I'm afraid to feel isolated from him." This anxiety is typical of couples who are close in most other ways, and it tends to abate when they learn to concentrate on where they converge rather than where they diverge.

There is no simple solution to their predicament, but I suggested that a serious discussion of their suppressed feelings was long overdue. This thoughtful, funny, devoted couple should certainly be able to find a way to talk about how they interact, and how they can each make efforts to express their opposing views while communicating respect for the other person's position.

However, in order for that to work, they have to feel it. She needs to temper her outrage that he disagrees (and understand why it's so intense) by figuring out why she cannot bear anything but total agreement with her spouse. He needs to temper his irony, stop bending over backward to avoid controversy, and overcome his fear that expressing his opinions means the end of their bond. This could actually relieve some of the tension, because avoiding rather than acknowledging takes more energy than they realize. If they cannot do this, they need to find another strategy, since the one they are currently pursuing is doomed to failure. Talking partisan politics exclusively with the like-minded is one solution, and there are plenty of opportunities to do so online or with friends and colleagues. Now he walks on eggshells while she retreats resentfully (when she doesn't explode) and feels depressed and inadequate. Neither of them trusts that the admiration and empathy they feel for each other in every other area of their lives will see them through.

But it would.

2

Young and Foolish

Couples who have been together for years settle into a style of political combat, even if it's a destructive and disturbing one. But younger people, or those in new relationships, have yet to do so, and the fights they have early on can be quite spectacularly awful. The good news is that they don't have a long history together to undo, and they can learn from experience what not to do. It's surprising, and encouraging, to see how frequently these couples can self-correct.

Political altercations that turn physical are the most wounding, leave the worst scars, and are the most difficult to resolve. Serious screaming, frontal attacks, and raw aggression—which often involve alcohol—were exclusively combat styles of millennials, among the people I interviewed. "We used to get under one another's skin the most when we sat down to dinner and had a few glasses of wine—that prompted the worst fight we ever had," said one thirty-five-year-old woman, reminiscing about the early days of her marriage to a man more conservative than she is. Nobody I spoke to who was in a long relationship ever broke things or shoved, pushed, or wrestled with a mate, or even slammed a door as younger people did, and most older couples battled stone-cold sober. As bruising as their wars were, they were wars of words.

However, my younger informants, despite their impetuousness and lack of inhibition, were also more forgiving and resilient, as well as surprisingly frank and self-aware. They seemed less self-righteous and, mostly, more open-minded than the older couples, and their willingness to figure out their own contribution to the argument was considerably greater. Their attitudes seemed less entrenched, and their patterns of relating were not yet carved in stone. The way they talked to each other as they struggled to make up showed a sincerity and forthrightness that compensated for their lack of experience.

A dating couple, two close friends, and two gay partners, all under age thirty-five, fought over politics in dramatically different ways—sometimes verbally, sometimes physically, sometimes by misusing technology—but there were striking similarities in some of the causes, and the resolutions, of their battles.

Civics 101

Charlie,* a nineteen-year-old British fashion model, and Nicole,* his thirty-one-year-old girlfriend,† who is an American-born photographer with a black mother and a Norwegian father, had just moved in together, several months into their relationship, when they had a blow-up that could have destroyed everything. They were standing in the kitchen of their apartment when Charlie, infuriated by the racket their young neighbors were making by setting off firecrackers in the street in the middle of the night, said, "Why do poor black kids always make so much noise?"—a remark guaranteed to offend Nicole's sensitivities. Even though she knew that Charlie was no racist, she proceeded to give him an impromptu lecture on race relations in America. "He said something that crossed the line," she explained. "So I had to go into the history of slavery, I referred to films—I wanted to give insight to this young white privileged male." The young white privileged male—who had actually grown up with a single mother in straitened circumstances—was having none of it. "Did it change your mind?" I asked Charlie. He answered with a smile and an abrupt, defiant "No."

---

† An asterisk indicates the actual first name of someone who participated in the "I Love You, But I HATE Your Politics" podcast and was referred to by name there.

Nicole took Charlie's outburst—and his annoyance at her attempts to indoctrinate him—very personally, because her parents had experienced serious discrimination. "He was dismissive, he wasn't receptive. I didn't feel I was getting through," she said—having no clue that nobody in his position would appreciate being forced to submit to a "lecture," the verbal equivalent of having an article thrust in your face. No matter how heartfelt and legitimate her motivation, the tone was off, and the know-it-all attitude with which she conducted his "education" rubbed him the wrong way. Had she tried instead simply to express and explain her own feelings, rather than instructing him like a mother or a teacher, he might well have listened. Instead things deteriorated into a mutual shoving-and-yelling match:

NICOLE: I cornered him and forced him to sit down.

CHARLIE: She pinned me in the chair.

NICOLE: He tried to change the subject, and I felt I hadn't made my point. I wore him down.

CHARLIE: I was in her face, and that's what I was waiting for. I told her, "You don't need to think I'm right, just understand. Don't try to control what I have to say."

Then, in our interview, as if by magic, they began to listen to each other and to communicate what they felt. Charlie, acknowledging his ignorance and concerned about the unintentional pain his remarks caused her, said, "I appreciate I don't know the cultural context enough to comment, but I need to know that what I said didn't really offend you." His openness and sensitivity to her feelings allowed Nicole to explain that her superior stance came from her own anxiety: "Unless I know you feel some compassion for others, how could you feel compassion for me?" Once goodwill was reestablished, Nicole was able to recognize why her approach failed and to express eloquently what she needed from him: "I was belting you with facts. You're allowed to have your opinions. I just want you to conduct yourself with grace." This admonition he willingly accepted.

They also learned something important about each other that should prove useful in resolving the inevitable battles they will have in the future. As a result of discussing their first big fight and the subjective meanings it had for each of them, Charlie realized that his mother "brought me up to be straightforward and speak my mind," while Nicole recalled that she had been warned all her life by her mother to "watch what you say." One was encouraged not to be careful, and the other always to be careful. Now, beyond the heat of the moment in which everybody is deaf and blind, they could hear and see and feel for each other. Empathy transforms communication and fosters intimacy, whether the topic is politics or anything else.

Reeducation, or How to (Almost) Lose Your Best Friend and Influence Her Not at All

Charlie and Nicole employed brute force and raised voices to drive their points home, and almost wrecked their relationship in its early days as a result; Rachel* employed cutting-edge technology for the same purpose, and came close to fatally alienating Brittany,* her best friend for seven years, which is a very long time when you are both twenty-five. The mutual goodwill they had accrued over those years—and their eventual willingness to talk about the dangerous rift that Rachel's indoctrination campaign brought about—prevented the discord from becoming permanent.

Brittany always thought of Rachel, her sorority sister and confidante, as "great fun," and she was touched by her warmth and heart as well. When they both moved to New York City for work, they had so much to talk about—they texted each other every nanosecond—that the political chasm between them never became an issue until the run-up to the 2016 election, that vortex in which so many worthwhile relationships foundered. Rachel was a passionate Hillary supporter who had canvassed for her candidate in the South. Brittany had worked as a Republican intern on Capitol Hill, which had dampened her zeal and erased any wish to participate in government. Brittany's big mistake in 2016 was to inform Rachel that she was so disgusted with both presidential candidates that she had decided not to vote—something that Rachel found unacceptable. What followed could very well have spelled the end of a beautiful friendship.

One day that July, after both nominating conventions had decided on their standard-bearers, Brittany looked at her phone and found a remarkable email from Rachel. It was a PowerPoint presentation. The subject line was "Re-education," and the title was "Great Shit Hil Has Done." Rachel, in her missionary zeal to convert her friend not only into a voter but into a staunch Democratic one like herself, had sent Brittany a jaw-dropping document. It went beyond touting her candidate's virtues and accomplishments in detail: there was also a section entitled "Donald's Accomplishments," which was, of course, blank.

The recipient of the unsolicited reeducation effort was understandably furious and saw it as bullying, not enlightening. This made the "lecture on the history of slavery in America" that Nicole foisted on Charlie look subtle.

Brittany's initial response didn't help. "I sent her back a snarky email about how much Hillary was hated," she recalled. "I asked, 'Who's the taller of the midgets?'" But, Brittany noticed that, other than a couple of long, serious rebuttals and yet more policy stats, Rachel wasn't answering any of her attempts to get back in touch. Unlike what many other millennials would have done, Brittany had sensibly refrained from telling Rachel how she really felt via text and was asking to meet in person.

Luckily for their friendship, Brittany did not give up, despite Rachel's retreat into radio silence mode for months, always claiming to be "too busy" to meet her. When I asked Rachel why she had not responded to these repeated overtures, she told me, with insight and regret, that she was "highly conflict-averse," and that she probably would have let the rift become permanent if Brittany had not doggedly continued to pursue her. Clearly Rachel hadn't seen her PowerPoint as anything objectionable, since in her mind it simply presented objective truths—as if she were Thomas Jefferson stating in the Declaration of Independence, "Let facts be submitted to a candid world." People older and more experienced than she have been known to behave similarly, with similar results; browbeating has never converted anybody, yet it continues to be the method of choice for many.

I wanted to understand what possessed her to send such a manifesto. "Maybe I should have done it in person," she mused, "though I don't regret doing it. It's my life goal to get her to believe in something." But in fact it was clear that her real goal was to have her friend believe in what *she herself* believed in. "Brittany's passivity isn't grown-up," Rachel said. "She says, 'I don't need to be involved,' but I say, 'That's insane—how can you not have an opinion? How can you not be voting for Hillary?'" However,

Rachel also said that if Brittany came to espouse conservative opinions, "I couldn't be her friend; the way people engage with politics is a manifestation of their core beliefs"—a debatable assertion that I heard from people on both sides of the aisle who were similarly convinced that they alone had a lock on truth.

The real root of the conflict between these two young women was far deeper than whom to vote for, or even whether to vote; it had to do with different psychological interpretations of the meaning of political engagement. For Rachel, it was essential to be an activist so she wouldn't feel she was suffering passively in her own life; her parents had been gravely ill simultaneously, and she gathered strength, she told me, from human rights advocacy and from promoting the Democratic Party's agenda. It was her source of consolation in adversity. "My ability to have strength and be OK is to realize that humans everywhere go through trials and I have the agency to do things in this world," she explained. She saw her PowerPoint as "part of my duty as a citizen to inform others." Her admonitions had quite a different meaning for her friend, whose own parents had dictated how she was to feel and react in family crises, which were always supposed to take moral precedence over her own emotions and needs. The two friends were on a collision course, rooted in their own pasts, that neither was aware of.

Ultimately, Brittany valued Rachel more than she was

furious at her, and Rachel felt the same way. "We've always had an honest relationship," Brittany told me. "We go to each other with problems. At the end of the day, I trusted her." Rachel agreed that her friend had faithfully stood by her in a crisis—surely as compelling an indication of character as how she voted.

Finally, Brittany got through to Rachel. She confronted her friend directly one night when they were attending the same party and insisted that they discuss what had happened. She wasn't going to lose a real friendship over politics. This time Rachel responded: "I told her, 'I didn't mean to put you out in the cold, and I apologize,'" she said. Now they are closer than ever—even though Rachel had to add, "I hope you're becoming less of a Republican."

Brittany, ever the realist, knows that she may well not have seen the last PowerPoint she'll ever get from Rachel—after all, the full title of the one she got was "Great Shit Hil Has Done, Part 1." Even though Rachel's preferred candidate will not be running for president in 2020, Brittany knows that Trump most likely will be. "If he runs again it'll happen again," she told me with amused resignation. With the necessary updates and a revised title, "Part 2" may then be winging its way to her in-box in 2020—but by then both sender and recipient should be older and wiser, and able to handle the fallout differently because, as they said in unison, "now we both realize what important friends we are for each other."

The War Between the Trump Supporters

You know something is seriously amiss when one avid pro-Trump conservative is so furious that he calls another Trump supporter "a liberal" in the heat of an argument. Neither one of them remembers very clearly what the most recent installment of their ongoing feud was about, but voices were raised, a marble table was broken, and a cell phone got smashed. Peter Collins, a thirty-year-old television producer, and Jake Johnson, a thirty-five-year-old advertising executive—smart, charming, savvy young men who have been together five years—periodically battle over some political issue or other. On this particular occasion, the name-calling and demolition derby was followed by a fistfight and culminated in a wrestling match (fortunately, no serious physical consequences ensued). The rest of the time they are an affectionate, responsible, and civic-minded couple.

Similar mayhem has transpired between them more than once before, despite the fact that they are virtually on the same page ideologically, vote for the same candidates in both federal and state elections, and have similar perspectives on the world in general.

Their alcohol-fueled disputes ("We come to blows—alcohol helps," Peter admitted), and the collateral damage to objects and psyches, have diminished significantly over the last six months, but such over-the-top reactions to disagreements that would strike a bystander as trivial still lurk under the surface of their relationship. Something deeper must underlie these bouts, as is the case with the majority of intense, protracted fights ostensibly about politics.

Peter and Jake both back the forty-fifth president, but for different reasons, and this disparity ostensibly provokes their arguments, although it is not the fundamental cause of them. Jake was a passionate fan from the beginning. "I understand Trump," he asserts. "What people can't see is that he's calculated, not impulsive." Peter supports Trump's policies but deplores his personality, especially his treatment of women. Their dueling perspectives are a major point of contention between them because each wants the other to accept, if not convert to, his own point of view—just like couples whose opinions are much further apart than theirs.

Why do their essentially minor disagreements become combustible? Their divergent styles of dealing with conflict, and the meaning to each of them of the way the other reacts—especially what gets stirred up from each one's past—are the sources of the problem.

"Our ways of fighting are different," says Jake. "He's loud, aggressive, screams at the top of his lungs. I try to be calm and factual, but he cares about volume, not facts. I mention a hundred thousand facts, then he gets drunk and I get even more factual. Then we throw things at each other. Luckily, we've calmed down quite a bit by now."

Jake—who was Peter's much-admired mentor when they first met—subscribes to the Nicole and Rachel School of Pedagogy when they fight, and his efforts elicit similar responses.

Of course, Peter has his own take on the proceedings. "Jake makes feelings into facts. When I bring up Trump's character flaws, he says, 'That's not true, you don't know.'" Has Peter assumed that his former mentor is more authoritative than he actually is? "Here I am thinking he's the smartest person I know—then I think, maybe he's not so smart. I can't stand when the other person doesn't listen." He wants Jake to accept that they actually disagree on this important issue and to recognize that his own opinion is legitimate. "What if what's really happened is that I've just realized we really do have core differences? I understand there can sometimes be no agreement, and I'm not going to give in on this." This, however, does not sit well with Jake. "If I say, 'I'm not changing my mind,' he won't shut up. Jake doesn't stop. I want to move on, but he's still digging. When I leave the room, he follows me out of the room—he's got to get through. It's like verbal rape."

The shocking simile Peter chooses indicates how traumatized Jake's intrusive behavior makes him feel. Extreme reactions like his, which are disproportionate to the current situation, usually have roots in personal history.

As a child, Peter felt profoundly repudiated by his distant and authoritarian father, who, before he divorced Peter's mother, always sided with his three sisters in arguments, never with him, and rejected his son for disagreeing with him politically; Peter's independence of mind was never a source of pride. "He told me to apologize to my sisters, but I said, 'No, they're in the wrong'—and of course I was the one who got punished," Peter recalled, still smarting. He hated his father's arbitrary, irrational conduct. "Lack of intellect still makes me lose it," he said. His opinions and principles were never respected, and even now he cannot bear not being heard. When he feels erased and shamed by Jake, he has to assert himself verbally or—when really desperate and pushed too far—physically.

In fact, Jake's extreme persistence in maintaining contact with Peter when they fight stems more from profound separation anxiety and desperation than from bullying. Jake spent much of his childhood hospitalized with severe eczema and allergies. "I was left out of everything," he recalled. He must have interpreted being removed from his family as banishment and rejection, as any child in his lonely and frightening situation would.

Even when Jake was home, his father was unavailable physically and emotionally. His parents were alienated from each other, and his father spent much of his time in his den in the basement, where his mother "just let him be." When Jake's parents fought, his father shouted, retreated there, and got drunk often enough that his mother "forced" him to go to AA. These are the reasons why Jake has such a profound fear of being abandoned that he has to follow Peter out of the room when they fight. He cannot bear to be separated, even by a door between two rooms, and Peter's angry exits evoke panic in him.

When they fight, each of them unconsciously becomes the other's unresponsive, rejecting, judgmental, or combative father. Each feels erased by the other and has to make himself known by any means necessary. These experiences from childhood still provoke rage and anxiety, with underlying sorrow that feels unendurable.

In order to fend off the next blow-up, Peter tries, often unsuccessfully, to defuse arguments by taking the blame in advance. "I acknowledge I'll be the intemperate one. I'll say, 'You know my temper—I'll end up breaking something,'" he warns Jake. But they are beginning to understand the dynamics and, more importantly, the sources of the behavior that make both of them feel terrible. "Luckily, we're learning to shut this down," Peter notes with relief.

One thing that is making a difference is that they are generous in their appreciation of each other, something neither of them ever got from his father. Referring to their joint civic accomplishments—they participate in local politics—Peter says, "Jake and I compete, but we work so well with each other. As much as we fight, we've done spectacular things together."

The most hopeful sign of all is that both of them are figuring out where their uncontrollable emotions come from and what unfinished business each evokes in the other—and eliminating drinking from the mix. Jake says, "Our fights stem from politics, but they bring up underlying issues of what's wrong between us. Without alcohol we'd hardly be fighting." Peter adds, "It's not Trump that destroys relationships—it's the people in the relationship; Carville's still with his wife." Independently, they each admitted, "The things we fight about are so stupid."

Once it really sinks in that politics is the mere veneer of their anger at each other, they can deal with the real sources. Their mutual admiration, basic like-mindedness, and ability to understand psychology bode well for the future—if they can resist the impulse to act everything out on the furniture and each other's bodies.

The threat of one calling the other "a liberal" in the heat of the moment may never go away. But as much as it rankles, a hyperbolic verbal slight can be overlooked, or even deflected with humor because it is so absurd. That damage is a lot easier to repair than the fallout from fistfights or broken tables, phones, and hearts.

⁂

Growing up is hard to do, but it is gratifying to see how many younger couples, no matter how deep their distress or the magnetic pull of pain from the past, manage to do it.

3

Family Feuds I

Parents vs. Children

Political fights between blood relations are the most deeply rooted of the genre because they are the original editions, not contemporary copies. Emotional connections with parents, siblings, children, and other close relatives cannot be severed; you can't get a divorce from your family of origin even if you leave town or change your name, your religion, or your party affiliation, because these relationships live within us and inform all other intimate bonds for the rest of our lives.

It can be something as subtle as a disapproving look or a negative comment, or as out there as being unfriended by your parent or sibling on Facebook, having your invitation to a family holiday celebration rescinded, or becoming persona non grata with your own relatives because of your voting preferences, that causes tensions to escalate, sometimes uncontrollably. Any of these things can lead to lasting estrangement that becomes increasingly difficult to undo if ignored or left to fester. In every case, something more fundamental than ideological conflict is going on.

The most recalcitrant and distressing of all family altercations occur between parents and children. They are the oldest and the deepest, and have the longest backstory, which has nothing to do with their overt subject matter and everything to do with issues of love, identity, acceptance, self-expression, and autonomy. These are the fights that provoke the most intense distress and feelings of helplessness, and even of doom. Children—including grown ones who have children themselves—despair of getting through to mothers and fathers, and, in some poignant cases, parents feel shut out of their children's lives; all of these primordial struggles are acted out in the political arena. The specific news-related content and party affiliations of the combatants vary, but the emotions are numbingly repetitive and leave the participants feeling paralyzed, victimized, and utterly unable to get any perspective on what is going on, let alone to recognize their own part in perpetuating the conflicts—a piece of knowledge that is essential in order to change the outcome.

Why are political brawls the form these struggles take? The partisan content is often so compelling and makes people so shortsighted that it's hard to identify the underlying themes. Media furor legitimizes and stokes the rage—and masks its real sources. Authentic differences of opinion are only the excuse for attacks that cannot and should not be tolerated. Politics, especially these days, is a convenient medium for expressing a multitude of emotions; the closer the relationship, the more there is to fight about.

Political fights also add a whole new dimension to coping with an aging or impaired parent. The pain and anxiety such tragic situations evoke make adult children cling tightly to surface disagreements because if they looked underneath they would have to face the inevitable prospect of disintegration and loss—and the recognition that they will never be able to fix the problems that have bedeviled these relationships for years. The most painful fight of all is the one in which the person you are desperate to reach no longer exists.

Of all efforts to change another person's mind, trying to transform an aging father or mother from an adversary to a comrade, or attempting to conduct a rational discussion with a parent who has become irrational, is the most fraught, the most hopeless, and the one in which it is hardest to admit failure.

Since political agreement has come to symbolize emotional harmony, it becomes more urgent to resolve conflicts as time is running out. Very often, adult children see this elusive goal as their last chance to get what they have never managed to get before. Facing that you can never be appreciated or accepted in your own right is so hard to tolerate that people prefer beating their heads against the wall of the other's emotional or physical deafness to admitting defeat. However, to renounce hope for success in this doomed endeavor is healthy and liberating, an essential step in accepting the unalterable limitations of the relationship. Terminating the fighting begins the grieving process while a parent is still alive.

Partisan conflict evokes and justifies strong emotions, providing a compelling external distraction from fear and anger about illness, aging, and mortality, and this explains the frightening, disturbing intensity of some of these encounters. Some people reported that their spouses and the other parent actually had to intervene to prevent fights from becoming physical.

In several cases, however, there was an unexpected benefit from an interview: it prompted the adult child to enlist the family in getting medical or psychological help for the combative parent—and, in one case, for the parent himself to seek help. Things improved considerably as a result.

"To raise the subject of politics in our family is to throw dynamite"

Few things are more painful than seeing a beloved, admired parent aging badly. Still, children persist in trying to have political discussions in the hope of getting through, communicating about the world, making contact. Persistence is a setup for profound disappointment, but it is nearly impossible to abandon this strategy because of what that would imply: the death of hope. The possibility for rational discourse is long gone, but the longing for it is still desperately clung to.

Meghan Black's father has always been her inspiration. However, a variety of infirmities have now transformed the personality of this sixty-six-year-old scientist and contorted his mental rigor into enraged dogmatism, which he turns on her as well as on her three siblings, causing them all to feel anguished and desperate.

Meghan, a thirty-eight-year-old architect, proudly considers herself a chip off the old block. This imposing man—"He was always my go-to model for intellectual honesty," she told me—taught her to think, to question, and to back up her opinions with well-considered knowledge. But those days are past; now he turns on her no matter how hard she tries to reason with him, soothe him, or deflect his violent, insulting outbursts, and she is beside herself. "While I have felt equal to most complex problems of my adult life, this one, I confess, has me over a barrel," she says.

Even though she still admires him, she has no illusions about the sharp edges of her father's personality, which has always been difficult as well as impressive. "He's brilliant," she asserts, still clinging to the present tense. "We both have advanced degrees and common interests. Our relationship is characterized by a healthy respect for each other's intellect. However, he was always an authoritarian disciplinarian, and compromise has never been his strong suit."

Despite their similarities, Mr. Black is a lifelong conservative Republican, and she tacks left. His declining physical and mental health have caused discussions of ideological differences that were once occasions for stimulating intellectual sparring to degenerate into nightmares of pain and grief for everyone in the family, and for Meghan in particular. "To raise the subject of politics in our family is to throw dynamite," she says sorrowfully. "It provokes his worst tendencies and most extreme reactions. Now any disagreement indicates lack of respect for him." The strain on their relationship has become so severe that she has had to distance herself from the man she esteems most in the world: "It's harder to be his daughter as an adult than as a child, and we don't talk frequently anymore. Most wrenching by far is that I see this transformation in somebody I always thought had a unique approach to life." Can anything be salvaged?

The Black family's battles inevitably follow a numbingly similar trajectory that Meghan finds impossible to interrupt or alter. The family vows to avoid the patriarch's wrath by sidestepping politics completely, but it never works: "It's no problem if you share his beliefs, but it degenerates when we raise rebuttals—somebody inevitably starts down that road, and he gets like a dog with a bone."

Why, I ask, do they persist in "raising rebuttals" when the outcome is predetermined? "It feels dishonest not to try to set the record straight," Meghan explains—continuing to adhere to the precepts she learned from him as though he were still the rational, admirable opponent of her youth. "All I can hear is his voice in my head saying, 'Have you thought about this further?' I so totally want my father to be the person I remember." She recognizes the tragic change but cannot accept it yet.

The fights that mar Meghan's family gatherings are virtually identical to every one described to me by other adult children in her predicament. Holiday celebrations are the worst, a guaranteed catastrophe when a parent who has retreated into his or her own tormented world lashes out and visits frustrations on close relatives. Still, the Blacks hope for the best, which never comes. "We've been trying to take a steadier tack," Meghan says. "Every time we say, 'This one's gonna be good.'"

This Christmas, she thought she had come up with a fail-safe solution to avert a repetition of the demoralizing Thanksgiving they had endured. "We're going to a different location right down the street from where he lives so he won't be so exhausted by the four-hour trip to my house," she announced. "That way he won't be so irritable"—as though this would magically improve his mood and behavior.

Meghan and her family are proponents of what I call "the Geographical Solution"—the conviction that a change of venue can produce a change of mind. Despite its continued popularity with innumerable others besides the Black family, it has never worked yet.

At the end of our interview, I asked Meghan whether she ever dreamed about her father. She was surprised by the question and responded in the affirmative:

> As a kid I had a vivid dream about him. He'd died—this was his funeral. He's lying in the casket. Then he gets up and walks down the aisle—and goes to the pulpit to deliver his own eulogy! This dream said to me that things are always going to go the way he directs.

Even then she knew. This perceptive, amusing, and prescient dream told her that her father was so strong-willed and controlling that not even death could prevent him from having the last word—if not in person, then in her mind. She'd always understood this, but hadn't known that she knew.

Three months after our interview, I wrote to Meghan to ask how the new, improved Christmas celebration had gone. Her response was totally unexpected:

One of the things you mentioned really stayed with me. You said that the truth about his condition is something I can't bear. This is very true. I noticed it play out in large and small ways over the holidays. He was mercurial, confused, and controlling, punctuated by periods of near-maudlin sweetness and attention. He was generally calm, but it was an oppressive calm. We were all waiting for The Blow Up. We made it all the way to the end of my visit, when he began berating my brother's parenting decisions and how they reflected his liberal agenda politics.

The week after Christmas, my father voluntarily committed himself for psychiatric evaluation and treatment. Since then he has been seeing a psychiatrist and has added talk therapy to his regimen, which seems to be helping.

If I'm going to learn to bear my father's decline, I believe I need to limit my conversation to those things that let him be his best self. A discussion about the state of the world doesn't improve the state of our relationship. As he ages and his health deteriorates, I don't want to waste my time. That is my takeaway.

Both of them have made remarkable, and unexpected, changes. Mr. Black recognized his problem and sought help; his daughter renounced her fantasy of getting through to him and faced the reality of what is now possible in their relationship. This allows father and daughter to have something authentic for whatever time they have left together.

My Mother, the Leftist Automaton

Christopher Drake is convinced that his eighty-two-year-old mother has been brainwashed by the vast left-wing conspiracy. "She's a far-left RINO"—Republican in Name Only, for those unfamiliar with this lingo—"who gets all her news from *The New York Times, The New Yorker,* and NPR," the "libertarian, very conservative" fifty-eight-year-old retired contractor proclaimed. He sent me pages of meticulously transcribed verbatim tirades from her as proof—and added a few tirades against her tirades into the bargain. Though it is doubtful that the liberal media actually inspired her outbursts, they certainly were outrageous—provocative, insulting, and calculated to make her son feel furious, wretched, and ashamed of disagreeing with her, which they had clearly succeeded in doing. Since they live together, the opportunities for near-continuous vitriolic exchanges are boundless. Regardless of the topic—abortion, race, the NRA—she seemed always to be searching for news hooks to hook him with, and she was always successful, because he always tried strenuously to defend himself. Why can't he stop rising to the bait?

Pain and sorrow underlay his own ranting tone when describing hers. "The awful tone of political 'discussions' my mom and I have is wholly separate from our other interactions," he asserted, although, given the relentlessness of her attacks, I doubted it. "It's only when politics comes up that she cannot be spoken to or reasoned with. Why does she goad me as a racist/bigot/sexist/etc.? How can she ascribe such foul thoughts to me? Can it be possible that the single action of my vote for Trump is more indicative of my true character than my entire upbringing at her hands? Has she become a leftist automaton? How did she become so brainwashed by the left that she can say things to me like 'I'm glad your father is at rest so he doesn't have to see what you've become'?" He takes the bait every time, and thinks he has no choice but to do so, blaming her vitriol on the nefarious media and insisting that "modern liberalism is a mental disorder" instead of recognizing that her pathology goes deeper than any ideology, no matter how alien to his own. If he could blame *The New York Times* and its ilk for poisoning her mind and turning her against him, then she wasn't responsible; he convinced himself that if he tried hard enough and his arguments were compelling enough, he still might be able to recover her love and esteem.

Mrs. Drake was never the idolized moral authority for her son that Meghan Black's father had been for her, although Christopher was clearly still attached to his mother and labored to present her in the best possible light. She believed in education, he told me, and had an advanced degree herself. However, he did admit that "our childhood experiences were somewhat limited," which sounded like quite an understatement: although they were middle class, the Drakes took only "one or two" family vacations, he and his sister never had birthday parties, and his mother sounded severely obsessional, bordering on paranoid, about traveling by car, encountering bad weather, and other expectable hazards of living. Despite his positive spin— he insisted that "we knew kids who were far worse off than we were"—she came across as a killjoy, desperate to control everyone and everything around her; age and incipient memory loss had done nothing to improve her disposition.

Christopher painstakingly reported his strenuous efforts to reason with his "vicious, uncritical leftist" mother, no matter how outrageous her accusations. When I asked him to describe their exchanges, he said, "I was five words into my rebuttal before she screamed . . ." "Why on earth," I asked him, "do you try to rebut your mother when you know she'll never listen? Her opinions seem to be set in stone." "I don't look at it like this," he said, though with a smidgen of curiosity. "She'll be saying something and then she'll start shouting at me." "Are you hoping to find chinks in her armor?" I wondered. "What would it mean if there really were no way in?" "Then we couldn't talk about politics," he answered, crestfallen at the loss of connection and the failure of nerve that would represent. He would have to renounce hope of ever having the stimulating dialogue with his mother that he longed for, the one that would bring them closer. He could never get her to know him.

As we spoke, Christopher began to have an inkling that their wounding confrontations might have less to do with evil influences and more to do with issues in their relationship and with his mother's unrecognized mental problems. He volunteered that politics might not in fact be the only source. "I have a friend who is pretty hard left, and we can talk, we've remained close," he said—thereby contradicting his demonic-possession thesis, but opening up the possibility of insight into the real causes of these excruciating mother-son brawls.

I suggested that their arguments might be identical if the tables were turned: if she were a fanatical conservative on a rampage and he were a rational liberal seeking dialogue or understanding. This observation led him to recall a telling conversation he'd had with his late father—who his mother had insisted would be horrified over his son's right turn. "After forty years of being married to my mother, my father told me in confidence, 'I don't know why we're still married. Pushback is impossible; you can't fight her.' He went around her—and traveled by himself—but he never stood up to her. He was emasculated." "This is why you can't walk away from these fights with your mother," I said. "You'd be like him if you did."

I asked Christopher if he had ever dreamed about his father, and he recounted a dream that further explained his own reluctance to walk away: "I went into some random little pizza place, and there he was at a table working on papers. I was amazed to see him. I said, 'Dad, what are you doing here?' I knew he was dead." This was a man with a successful career who had run for public office; the degrading position in which Christopher placed him in his dream reflects his assessment of his father's character—that he deadened himself while he was alive by capitulating to his wife and failing to protect his son. In a second dream, Christopher's father was "off to the side," rather than center stage—another physical image of his emotional stance in life.

Talking about these dreams further opened Christopher's eyes and altered his understanding of why he felt compelled to hang on for dear life when his mother attacked his character in the guise of politics. "To think of your fights as politically motivated," I told him, "is taking you down the wrong road. It's what psychologists call the 'manifest content'—the surface material that conceals what is really going on. You've been thinking that if you refuse to engage, she would win."

I was impressed and moved by his response: "I will do what my father didn't do—I will take charge of the situation. There's a subtle difference between giving in because I'm weak versus I'm not going to start up with her because I'm strong."

Then he had another insight. "If we don't talk about politics, we won't have fights—." But he stopped himself. "Oh no, this is not true. I remember a nonpolitical fight when she almost threw me out of the house. I wanted to bake something, and I was going to borrow the pan I needed from my sister, but Mom insisted I should buy it immediately and gave me the money. She said, 'How dare you defy me?'" These, I suggested, were pretty strong words to use about a pan, and Christopher understood. "To realize that there's something very wrong with her is comforting," he said, the partisan outrage gone from his tone.

It is possible to feel pain and liberation at the same time.

Fathers and Sons

What do a thirty-four-year-old gay moralist techie, a thirty-one-year-old college dropout and Iraq veteran, and a twenty-three-year-old science-loving insurance salesman have in common? They all want their fathers to accept them despite radical political differences, and their longing falls on deaf ears.

These three sons try hard to keep the exchanges rational, find common ground, and avoid confrontations, but their fathers are bent on asserting their authority as well as their opinions, and things rapidly deteriorate. They do not seem to realize how much their dissenting sons admire them, or how hurt their sons feel.

Politics has become the final frontier for troubled father/son relationships—the perfect excuse for a fight that goes on forever. The techie's father floods his in-box with offensive group emails, the vet's father unfriended him on Facebook, and the salesman's father tries to physically assault him over opposing views on climate change. It makes no difference who is on the right or on the left; the pain is the same.

⚓

David Marshall, a thirty-four-year-old IT specialist, reads books on ethics and communication in his constant efforts to comprehend the gulf between him and his father. Both of them are well-educated men with mathematics degrees, but an ideological abyss yawns between them; David describes himself as a "gay, antiwar, pro-choice liberal" and his father as a "small-government, chicken-hawk Tucker Carlson fan who is also a semi-closeted racist." Although their arguments are heated, frequent, and bruising, he does not doubt his father's impressive intellect or that he and his father care about each other. "I've had to put up with his insane group emails for years, bloviating about some imaginary slight to the nation's integrity from the vile left," he told me, "and I'm shocked how someone so gifted could be so susceptible to propaganda, how someone with so little fear could be controlled so completely by it."

I was struck by his use of the phrase "I've had to put up with . . . ," which suggested to me that David thinks he not only has to tolerate receiving his father's obnoxious missives but also feels compelled to read them and to respond to them "with lots of appeals to reason," even though he admits they haven't seen eye to eye since he was fourteen years old, and that they have grown even further apart since then. "His ferocity surprises me," he said. "He can be cruel, and when he's wrong he's very good at saying why he's not." Even so, the compulsion to try to get through keeps David in the arena with an opponent he can never convince or prevail over.

Of all the people I interviewed, David had the most clearheaded understanding of what these chronic fights were really about. "Politics becomes a proxy battle for everything we cannot discuss—how we rub each other the wrong way, that we haven't lived up to each other's standards. Neither of us is being totally fair in our assessments, but we never talk about that directly," he admitted. "I don't believe that the details are as important as we would like to think." But his awareness does not help him resist the urge to mix it up with this man, who he says is "a contentious figure even outside the family," an observation many beleaguered children I spoke to made.

In the worst fight he can remember (although the details are long forgotten, as is usually the case), Mr. Marshall "got red in the face." Father and son were "throwing barbs at each other," but then, David said, "he reached out to me and we made up. Even if we hate the stupid things that come out of each other's mouth, there's something more to the relationship. I've never felt betrayed by him—that's why we keep it going. We're trying, even though we can't appreciate each other's arguments; there's nobility to having the other side expressed. I can't write off my father and the millions who agree with him." Not writing someone off, however, need not involve throwing barbs, or refighting the same unwinnable argument ad infinitum.

Having an impressive father abets fantasies of getting through, no matter what your experience has been. "I've dreamt of convincing him that the Democrats deserve to run things—I've thought that he could be swayed by rational argument, that he could see," David explained. But his hopes are repeatedly dashed: "He eggs me on and sends me those group emails—he can't resist. I get the sense he's itching for an argument." I got the sense that the father harbors similar fantasies of making the son see the light and considers his own arguments supremely rational, too.

David has devoted much serious effort to understanding his relationship with his father, but he has not addressed the most fundamental question: What compels him to read those enraging emails? "Why don't you say, 'Don't send any more of these to me?'" I asked. His answer is telling, poignant, and final: "Then he wins." I suggested that he needs to reconceptualize their interactions and change his goals. "You have to realize that reaching him is never going to happen, that you can never win," I said. "So I hold on to the idea that somehow I'll get through." "You're powerless to accomplish that," I said, "and you don't need to do it."

This idea began to make sense to David, demonstrating that he is not as closed-minded or intent on having his own way as his father is. "I see now it's more about me than about him—there's liberation in that." "It would be a weight lifted," I told him. "I get it—it's healthy to realize what you can and can't do. It's insane to be engaged like this all the time; it's becoming clearer."

From opposite sides of the political spectrum, he and Christopher Drake had the same revelation.

* * *

Mike Jones never fit into his family emotionally, academically, or ideologically—and he never will. He struggled with depression as a child and dropped out of college, but not for lack of ability. This thirty-one-year-old city official is deeply hurt that his parents, and his father in particular, do not appreciate his military career (he served multiple deployments in Iraq over seven years), or the legitimacy and seriousness of his political identity, which is the antithesis of theirs. "I keep trying to get through to them, but it's a hopeless case," he told me. "I never thought I could be on their level—I try to explain what I believe in and why, and they admit I have legitimate points, but they're back to the same arguments the next day. They're angry that I've not accepted their political views, and ignore that I've found my own facts and opinions."

This is a not-uncommon scenario between a father—he is the more verbally combative parent—on one side of the aisle (Mike's was a Reagan supporter who converted to the Democratic agenda) and a son on the other (he'd been sympathetic to the alt-right early on, still supports the NRA, and has become a deeply committed anti-Trump libertarian), but what torments Mike is that he is in awe of his rejecting parents, whom he calls "the two smartest people I've ever met." "Both have degrees in poli-sci," he said. "My dad is one of the most honorable, intelligent, and hardworking people. To be disliked so intensely by him is unbearable; it makes me feel helpless and backed into a corner."

Feeling out of sync with his family is nothing new for Mike—at this point, everybody else in it is a progressive—

but his brand of conservatism sent them over the top and caused his father to do the modern equivalent of writing him out of the will. "There is severe friction between us; he is quick to lump me with Trump, although I wouldn't vote for him for dog catcher. After several vicious back-and-forths about gun control, my dad unfriended me on Facebook. I never had screaming fights with him as a child, so it feels horrible that we're having them now."

In fact, the family fights that Mike is embroiled in as an adult are the direct heirs to the ones in his childhood; sibling rivalry and his father's disapproval are the ongoing themes. His younger brother, who did well in school and has the same political views as their parents, was favored then and still is, by a father who does not tolerate differences in temperament or principle. Mike finds it unbearable that Mr. Jones does not consider him "a person empathic with suffering," because convictions alien to his own cannot be moral. "They all view me as a stereotype and don't care about me and my opinions," he said with more sorrow than bitterness. Being dismissed all over again for going his own way wounds him deeply because it is a replay of his traumatic rejection as a child. He cannot escape being the family outcast, nor can he give up his convictions, an integral and seriously considered part of his identity, of which he is proud.

Mike has tried on multiple occasions to tell his father

how he feels, but finds his father so deafened and blinded by ideology that he cannot see how passionately his son longs to be appreciated and accepted for the admirable man he has become, because according to Mr. Jones, only those on the left can be admirable. Mike is doomed, he believes, to be forever considered inferior morally as well as intellectually. Arguing about principles is the only way he knows to assert himself, although he realizes it is useless. He cannot even take comfort in the knowledge that he and his dad "are having the same fight he had with his own father"—proof that it has little to do with Mike except as a projective screen.

I was touched by the despair and longing in this man, whose opinions were so different from my own, yet legitimate in their own right, and cruelly dismissed by the people who owed him empathy even in the face of radical disagreement. I tried to show him that the issues he and his father battle about aren't the real problem but are merely the external manifestation of deeper issues, some of which even preceded Mike's birth. "Politics is a dead end between you and him," I said. "That has to be your starting point. And this is an emotional, not an intellectual, conflict."

Unlike many other adult children I spoke to, Mike knows very well that he cannot win any of these fights, but, like them, he still feels compelled to participate, because of what it would mean to walk away. "I get into political discussions even though I know better, that I should never do it. I have to see that I can't let go," he told me, thereby refuting his own intellectual or psychological inferiority with this insight. To my question about what letting go would mean, he said, "There are good and bad reasons: noble ones—that you should stand up for what you believe is right—and bad ones—an obsessive drive not to lose. If I get the last word, find the right cutting remark, I feel like I'm defying or changing their mind or their opinion of me." "The turning point will be when you accept that you've disappointed your parents through no fault of your own, and that there's nothing you can do about it," I said, believing that laying out the truth could set him free.

The metaphor Mike offered was unexpected, counter-intuitive, and compelling. He cited the plot of *WarGames*, a 1983 movie that recalled his military experience and was a striking metaphor for his predicament with his power-ful, brilliant, inaccessible father. "A computer whiz kid who's a lousy student hacks the Pentagon and inadvertently tells a supercomputer to launch missiles. He thinks he's playing a complex game, but actually it's a real-world ther-monuclear war. He can get the computer to stop only by loading up tic-tac-toe over and over until his opponent re-alizes that if two players have equal skill, neither can win, that it will always come to a draw. The only way to prevail is just not to play. So if I can't convince my parents that my beliefs are coming from a good place, how could I convince any human being on earth?" "Often," I observed, "our parents are the *last* people on earth who can see us as we are, because they have too much invested in their own views. There could be relief and success for you to stop the 'war' by actively refusing to participate like the kid in the movie, and instead put your efforts where they could actually make a difference." Mike understood. "That's a hope," he said. "It would improve my relationship with my parents, probably for sure—now I dread watching the news with them because then I'll hear their comments and have to respond. My dad and I actually share other interests."

Perhaps there can be authentic common ground when he finally refuses to play the game ever again.

⁂

Bob Franklin, a twenty-three-year-old insurance salesman, is worried about his father, and with good reason. Bob has been desperately seeking advice about how to deal with the disturbing changes in the man he has admired all his life, but who has become almost unrecognizable—violent, furious, irrational, wretched, and erratic. "Sometimes our arguments, which are all about issues of the day, cause my mom and wife to come running to defuse the situation," he told me. "It can be quite comical, but at other times I seriously worry about his mental health."

Politics, not surprisingly, is the tip of the iceberg in these fights, always initiated by his father; Bob is a liberal, and

Mr. Franklin has been a Trump supporter from the very beginning and is "a huge climate change denier." This is especially painful for Bob because his father introduced him to science as a child and bought him wondrous books about the solar system. "He's gone off the deep end," Bob reported with distress in his voice. "At age fifty-six he started carrying a gun to ward off terrorist attacks, screaming at his wife and son"—and being extremely, perennially angry at the world.

Some of these personality changes Bob attributes to serious health issues, including cancer and major heart surgery, which caused his father to become "a different person, with only hate radio to keep him company." It seemed to me that Bob's father felt helpless to control anything in his life, and had become paranoid, enraged, and terrified.

Mr. Franklin's sober intelligence had been an important model for his son. "He used to like to look at facts," Bob said, shocked at the change. "Now if we have a debate he'll never listen. I see him pushing back against the facts, and I don't like to think of my father as ignorant." "This doesn't sound like ignorance," I said. "It sounds like he's scared and angry and grasping at politics to gain some kind of control when he feels it slipping away in his life." This explanation confirmed what Bob already knew but was afraid to acknowledge. "I'm starting to realize that myself," he concurred, "but because I love him, I don't like seeing him that way."

Paradoxically, Bob was relieved by having his fears

about his father confirmed, and this knowledge showed him what to do: "I see I'm pushing him further and further away. Instead of pulling him out of his cave I'm just kicking him further into it, scaring him further into it. He's holding on for dear life—it's consuming his life. He weaves politics into just about everything, and the anger and vitriol come out at home with his family. You're suggesting that I try to face what's really going on, that he could be paranoid or starting to have Alzheimer's, when I thought politics was the cause." "It's the other way around," I said. "Politics is both a symptom and a refuge. It's a way of explaining his feelings to himself when nothing makes any sense to him anymore."

Bob provided a sad and infuriating example of his father's obsession, and the impossibility of circumventing it: "I got him an Xbox for Christmas last year because he likes to play video games—it's about tanks. All he said about it was 'Obama left tanks in Iraq'—referring to a capture of American equipment by ISIS. But this is a World War II game. When I shoot down his argument with the facts, he gets angry."

Why does Bob persist in trying to argue with his father's view of the world despite the evidence that it is impenetrable? Unwillingness to face a tragic reality, and an inherited oppositional tendency, prevent him from acting on what he knows. "I hate seeing him be so wrong," he said. "Stubbornness might also be part of this—I get that from my father. Even earlier in his life he used to say, 'Nope, nope, nope.'" I asked, "How would you feel if you accepted the situation?" His response was poignant and brief: "Heart-broken."

Bob's father sounded seriously depressed, paranoid, and perhaps cognitively impaired as well. "His opinions are the result of his emotional and physical state—they're symptoms, not causes," I told Bob.

"You're making me see that it's not a two-sided situation," he said. "It's actually 90 percent him and 10 percent me trying to get through. I'm more involved than I previously thought." I could hear the relief in his voice, even though what he was facing was grim.

Bob's revelation had an effect both he and I never thought possible. I wrote to him several months after we talked to see how things were going, and I was delighted to get the following response from him:

I'm happy to say that my dad allowed himself to listen to us, his family, and has started an anti-depressant regimen. He's made tremendous progress and it's like my old dad is back. He still holds very conservative beliefs but he's more accepting of others' viewpoints. He quit listening to hate radio. He's even taking a second look at climate change!

The son was able to pull his father out of his cave.

What is striking is that all three of these young men esteem their flawed but impressive fathers, and that they all desperately want to be seen and heard by them, and appreciated for who they are.

Despite how they have been treated, each of them continues to admire his father—for good reasons, in every case. These sons need to realize that avoiding political "discussions," which inexorably deteriorate into mentally and sometimes physically bruising arguments, by actively and decisively refusing to engage no matter how provoked, is the only way to have an authentic relationship with these complicated men. They are all well on the way to acting on this knowledge.

Daughters vs. Mothers

Partisan arguments between mothers and daughters—at least those who volunteered to discuss them—had a different quality than other parent/child fights. Disruptive emotions went underground and were quickly papered over. Ideological differences, which were as passionate as those between any other family members, provoked greater anxiety about damaging the bond or forfeiting the other's good graces. Both combatants frequently declared that they simply could not comprehend each other's political stance ("We didn't raise her to be like that," said one outraged mother; "but we're close in every other way," said a bewildered daughter) and had given up any discussion of issues or of their feelings about their interactions. Sons, by contrast, tended to persevere in trying to get through to their recalcitrant parents—or kept fighting openly with them. When two women disagreed, neither wanted to address any incendiary subject directly. There was an almost phobic avoidance of controversy—something more typical of women in general.

Feminine voices were rarely raised, but there was a good deal of mental pressure exerted subtly—eye-rolling, offhand remarks, disapproving glances. Of course, negative messages still got through loud and clear. Passive-aggressive behavior prevailed: one right-wing daughter bought her progressive mother a subscription to *The Wall Street Journal* in order to broaden her view of the world—a perspective her mother expressed no desire to alter. The daughter convinced herself that her mother had solicited this "gift." From the way the daughter described their conversation, it seemed to me that her mother was just going along with the offer to avoid tension, but the daughter took it as a personal affront when her mother later requested that the subscription not be renewed. Both of them seemed to me to be screaming silently at each other, but neither dared to pick up the signal.

Among women, threatening topics tend to get summarily dropped and never referred to again. But they rankle, and the wounds can be deep.

☀

Tracy Mayer and her mother are extremely close. "She's the first person I go to with any problem," the fifty-four-year-old financial planner, who is single, said. "We're very much alike, both outgoing people excited by life." Mother and daughter have a great deal in common (including conflict avoidance) and are "the very best of friends—except when it comes to politics."

Tracy's tone changes appreciably when we discuss this topic. "I'm a conservative who reads a tremendous amount about issues; I often read several articles about the same thing so I can really understand it. I didn't vote for Trump, but he has now sold me. My mom lives in a college town and gets all her news from NBC and the local liberal press. If I get a glance at her Facebook feed it makes my blood boil. It's not that she believes or agrees with everything she sees there, but that is her exposure, and it sinks in to such a level that she thinks it's OK or mainstream to hate the president and wish him dead."

I was struck that she bothered to "get a glance at" a site that would infuriate her so, especially since she knew in advance what she would find there. Typically, people who do this are looking for reinforcement, and perhaps justification, for views they already hold. She allows herself to feel outraged in private, and gets irate every time her covert glancing confirms the fact that she and her mother continue to disagree profoundly about something that matters deeply to her but that can never be broached.

Both Mrs. Mayer's views and her unwillingness to appreciate that her daughter's differ trouble Tracy. A critical remark her mother made in a political fight they had during the Obama years has stayed with her and has inhibited her from mixing it up with her mother ever since. "After a couple of glasses of wine, she said to me, 'You shove your opinions down people's throats.' I didn't want to be perceived as someone who's always angry and fighting. From then on I was afraid to say anything because I got that reaction. It hurt so bad that I didn't want to discuss it, so we acted like it didn't happen."

After that fight, Tracy's father advised her to be "more gentle" in her political discussions with her mother, and she thought she was heeding his advice. "That made me change the way I approached her—I became a lot more gentle. But she is never open to listening to me. I'm glad I have the values that I do, they're important to me. This is a part of me I want her to recognize. I'm not seeking her agreement; I'm seeking to be heard and to be respected—but even when I show her an article that explains something more fully than what she sees, she never concedes that she was misinformed."

Tracy's new approach was doomed to failure; her article-thrusting—she uses the euphemism "showing"—belied her assertion that all she wanted was for her mother to appreciate her position. Instead, she wanted her mother to see the light, confess her ignorance, and concede "the truth"; much of their conflict came from Tracy's obliviousness to what she was really up to. If she could admit her real goal to herself and stop her provocative behavior, she might actually be able to communicate better with the woman she loves and get what she needs from her, even if it is not everything she wants. Changing her mother's mind is impossible, but getting her attention and respect is within reach—a realistic aspiration.

In all the mother/daughter pairs I talked to, it was always the daughter who was the aggressor—even if the aggression was subtle and unacknowledged.[†] Mothers tended to lament that their daughters had strayed, but did not make strenuous or desperate attempts to get them back in the fold. Every daughter embroiled with her mother told me that all she wanted was to be appreciated, but her actions (offering unsolicited articles, buying subscriptions that had not been requested, hounding her mother to see things differently) showed that what she was really

---

[†] Not every politically conflicted mother and daughter behave like this, but I believe avoidance and passive-aggressive behavior are far more common with them than direct confrontation initiated by either side.

after was assent that her own views were right and her mother's wrong. Lockstep agreement, they all believed, was the only way they could be sure of their mothers' respect and appreciation. Daughters sought harmony and like-mindedness with their mothers and became anxious, and sometimes aggressive, when it was lacking. It was as though the only way they could feel secure in a mother's love was to see their own image reflected in her political views. This conviction, endemic among daughters, has come to infect many intimate relationships in the contemporary world.

It is telling that Tracy did not want me to interview her mother because "she may not realize how irritated I get with her," but I was sure Mrs. Mayer knew, and was avoiding confrontation as strenuously as her daughter. People who know each other as well as these two are familiar with what the other person's facial expressions, body language, and tone of voice convey. It is a comforting fantasy that suppressed intense feelings are not communicated nonverbally to another person, when in fact they are only harder to identify and address. Tracy also complained that her mother "never tells me what she thinks," but this does not mean Mrs. Mayer does not show her in other ways. The mother is as afraid of conflict as her daughter is, and just as entangled in it.

Politics, it turns out, is not the only hot-button issue that Tracy avoids bringing up with her mother for fear of the consequences for their relationship. She has never been able to address her mother's alcoholism—she referred to it obliquely when describing their Obama-era fight—even though it disturbs her profoundly, and even though she herself suffered from the same problem but has been sober for many years.

Tracy will never succeed in changing her mother's mind, but she could get her mother to listen seriously to her point of view if she stops lobbying her and simply states her own beliefs with no ulterior motive. I told her I believed that the authentic goodwill between them makes this possible but that she must take the risk to speak out.

Tracy wrote me an encouraging email after our interview:

> It would be a positive thing to say these things to my mother. I can bring this up with her. She doesn't have to agree—I just want her to listen. I want it to be known that I have opinions that I came by validly, it's who I am. I want her to tell me, "You can be different from me and I still think you're great." You helped me see that. I'm starting to get more courage to discuss things!

Dealing with the elephant—and the donkey—in the living room will have benefits for their relationship far beyond the voting booth.

The Prodigal Father

Seth Cantor, a sixty-year-old journalist and editor of an influential website that espouses and promotes conservative ideas, has always spoken his mind about politics, even if some of the important people in his life did not agree or appreciate his doing so. Over the years, he has alienated many liberal friends, colleagues, and family members not only by what he said but by how he said it. Although nobody doubted his eloquence, his grasp of the facts, or the intellectual clarity of his arguments, he could be single-minded, combative, and relentless. No relationship was exempt; he took his politics everywhere.

For years, Seth thought of himself as an embattled partisan whose responsibility was to explain, defend, and present the principles he passionately endorsed. It was incumbent upon him not only to disseminate conservative ideas through his website but to be a spokesman himself. Not surprisingly, this mission put him in conflict with those who did not want to engage in political debates or who had different convictions. He felt compelled to make his arguments as forcefully as possible—a style that can work on television or on the web, but goes over less well with one's friends and family.

As political discourse became ever more inflammatory in recent years, many of Seth's left-leaning friends, whom he had known for decades, turned on him. Some of them even accused him of helping to elect the president they abhorred because his website publicized and provided a forum for Trump's supporters—although he himself was not one of them.

Seth was devastated when people he had known intimately since high school summarily stopped speaking to him. "I'm still suffering because three or four old friends severed with me; history and a sense of community mean something to me. A very liberal guy with whom I'd been close for forty years shunned me. I really want to salvage that relationship—I have the impulse to contact him all the time, but I sense he's not ready." Another reason for holding off on attempting to reconcile with this outraged friend is that the friend may not be willing, and Seth may not want to risk another confrontation and rejection that could be irreparable. Losing people because of his beliefs and how he has championed them has left him lonely. "I find myself grieving more for lost friends than dead ones," he said.

Seth attributes his friends' rejection of him to the intensification of political conflict and the increasing intolerance for opposing views that surrounded Trump's election. "Trump is the irritant that turned everything into a moral litmus test," he said, and he was on the wrong side of morality for many of the liberals and progressives he knew. Estrangement from people he cared about disturbed him deeply—he had never severed a relationship over ideology himself—but he felt there was nothing he could do about it.

In the wake of these escalating losses, family relationships came to mean more to him than ever. So he was dismayed to realize that his political pronouncements, and how he delivered them, had dangerously alienated his own liberal elder daughter, and that their relationship was in serious jeopardy as a result.

Seth had sensed her growing antagonism for years, but now he noticed that she was actively avoiding contact with him and making angry, bitter comments every time they saw each other. "I felt like I was on the spot when we discussed politics," he said. "When she'd challenge me, my response was always very defensive—I'd try to explain everything." What the father imagined as a dialogue the daughter experienced as a harangue. She thought he wanted to convert her or override her opinions, when what she needed was for him to accept that they were legitimate even though they differed from his; this is a universal longing that goes beyond politics.

She was put off by his attitude as well as his ideas. "I could see the distress I was causing her because of my own temper," he said. "It's not anything she did, but my way of reacting, that caused the breach. The liberal onslaught on conservatism was escalating, and I was in the role of explaining and defending the right wing"—a role he had taken on in his own family as well as in the world at large.

Finally he recognized the damage he had done and took responsibility for his combative and opinionated behavior—behavior that many parents engage in though very few acknowledge. But what could he do about it? He felt desperate and helpless to avert a deeper breach that he feared was inevitable and that would devastate him for the rest of his life. Theirs was a bond he simply had to salvage. To do so, he knew he had to change, even if it meant altering what seemed like an essential part of his personality; the consequences of staying the same would be catastrophic for him and for his daughter.

Then she became pregnant with her first child, and this galvanized Seth into action. Protecting his ego, even though it might be justified with a friend, had no place with his own child. He had to try to repair the damage by any means necessary—and he decided that what was necessary was to eliminate any discussion of politics with her ever again.

Seth described the moment of truth. "She was trying to have a political discussion with me, but when she tried to get me to respect her position, I got defensive." He realized that his need to win arguments unconsciously extended to winning them with his own daughter, and decided then and there that he "would not allow anything to interfere with our relationship. I could lose her, and be excluded from her life. She needed to hear that our connection was more important than our political differences. I could do this only through actions, not words."

The last fight they ever had took a totally unexpected turn. "We were having a discussion, and it was going badly; I wasn't able to govern my reactions. I heard my voice getting louder, and I felt strangely detached from the things coming out of my mouth. I couldn't stand it. Then she said, 'I need you to stop,' and she went into her room. I followed her, I sat down, and I opened my mouth to talk—but instead of continuing the argument, I said, 'I'm afraid I'm going to lose you,' and I started to cry." For a man who always seemed to be in control, this was the most eloquent, anguished, and relatable thing he could have done—and it changed everything.

⁂

Many months have now passed. Seth has been true to his word, and his relationship with his daughter and her new family has flourished as a result. His attitude has changed dramatically, and not just about politics: "I don't feel that she has to be the one to call me—I understand it's incumbent upon me to make room for her, not the other way around. Politics is just not that important anymore. I'd rather talk about other things."

What he couldn't anticipate was that relegating politics

to a secondary place in his psyche would transform his life; he became more himself as a result. "I have let myself out of this position I was in. I realized how stressful it was for me to be a perennial spokesman—only now that I'm out of it can I see what a toll it took on me for so long; I don't want to play that role anymore." Instead of being the implacable Defender of the Faith, he has become a better father, and a more empathic—and happier—man.

4

Family Feuds II

Sibling vs. Sibling

Sibling disputes are the second-oldest fights in the world, only slightly less intense than parent/child battles, and politics is second only to dealing with aging parents and inequitable wills as the most popular subject of contention between brothers and sisters. Political battles between siblings are a convenient way to express every unresolved problem from their shared history, often without the combatants realizing what they are really fighting about. These altercations, which can be surpassingly bitter and lead to irreparable estrangement, are never simply objective disagreements about the president, the state of the nation, or who has the correct view of the world. Ancient themes of rivalry, competition, envy, and favoritism are right under the surface, ever present though ignored.

One of the subtle functions of these disputes is to transfer unfinished family business from parents to peers. They give adult brothers and sisters yet another chance to fail at winning the perennial battles that have bedeviled family life since Cain and Abel. However, if they are handled by the combatants with awareness and understanding, they can also offer opportunities to work through many lingering issues or to consciously put them aside—opportunities that are especially urgent and poignant, since siblings are usually the last family members alive and the only people who remember your childhood.

WASP vs. WASP

They had their own private language until they were five years old, and they look alike, even at age sixty-five, but there the Butler sisters' similarities end.

Laura Butler has all the characteristics of the classic WASP—a strong work ethic, civic-mindedness, suppression of emotion. She wholeheartedly espouses the right-wing agenda and voted enthusiastically for Trump. Susan, Laura's identical twin sister and ideological mirror image, has the same ingrained sense of community responsibility, but she is a forthright activist who speaks her mind and has powerful emotions, powerfully expressed—which is in itself a problem, given their heritage. Navigating their already-fraught relationship through contemporary politics is an ongoing struggle, which would be denied and conducted entirely sub rosa, if Laura had her way.

According to Laura, it must have been her sister Susan's years working in a nonprofit environment that turned her away from the staunch Republicanism of their youth, which she herself still upholds. "When you have a corporate career, and work in the computer world as I have, you become more objective," she asserted, as if this were a universally accepted truth. So confident is she in the correctness of her views that she assumes only malign external influences could have distorted her sister's judgment and political opinions—opinions that Susan told me were the fruit of carefully considered convictions.

Laura could not imagine that her sister could have legitimate reasons to see the world differently, which essentially makes any exchange about politics impossible, or so fraught with unacknowledged prejudices as to be enraging for Susan. The only way Laura can deal with their differences of opinion—which easily ignite unless they both exercise Herculean self-control—is by avoiding, denying, and suppressing any discord completely, or by making snide remarks that she can disavow. Her own feelings and judgments seep out more than she knows.

Since the twins live in the same town and see a great deal of each other, both by choice and by chance, avoiding clashes is not easy. As Laura sees it, "We avoid politics—

we get to a point and say we can't talk anymore. As soon as we realize it's getting a little confrontational, we back off. For instance, she's against Trump's anti-immigration policy, and I support it because we should take care of people here; when we try to discuss it we talk over each other. But," she insists, "there's not much anger; everybody's entitled to their opinion. I try to look at things from the other person's point of view. Since my corporate training is to explain, I rarely tell people what I think. In our family we're never allowed to say, 'You're wrong.' I go to great lengths not to disagree in any way—I do not want to trigger an argument." When I asked her how she keeps discussions with her sister from becoming heated, she offered the following example: "Once I was brutally honest and she walked off. I went back in, put my arm around her, and I said, 'You're my twin. I love you even when you're wrong'"—a true statement, but one that contradicted her prime directive, and that few people would find conciliatory. She seemed unaware of how condescending she was.

Susan has quite a different take on their interactions about politics, both pre- and post-Trump, and about other issues as well. While Laura insists that "other than Trump, we're on the same page all of the time," Susan recalls "heated discussions before Trump" that escalated dramatically after his election, as well as colliding worldviews in general. "We sure do have differences," she said emphatically. "When he won it was devastating for me, but my sister and her husband were happy about it. I was very disappointed by this on many levels. We can't have a discussion about it at all because it becomes very emotional." It is no easy feat to have a frank discussion on controversial matters when one person avoids and denies any negative feelings even as she is covertly expressing them.

Susan vividly recalled the particulars of a "horrible argument" that Laura did not mention. It was about immigration, which is her own personal flash point: "A woman with a diabetic daughter who had been living in our town for eighteen years was going to be deported. Her husband works hard, and had committed no crime. Because of my efforts she got to stay, but he did not. I brought up Trump's policy on this issue, which I vehemently oppose, with my sister and her husband, and they brushed it off—they feel it's his agenda and he's doing what he promised. I said, 'I hate Trump!' and she said, 'That's a very strong word.' Then I said, 'If there was a stronger word I'd use it'—and my sister told me I was being stupid. She accused me of becoming a Democrat because I took a course on social activism. She said, 'You're not listening to me,' and I replied, 'I'm listening to you—I just disagree with you.' This was the first time she realized I had different opinions."

Temperament is part of the problem when one twin is a progressive sympathizer and a provocateur who cannot avoid speaking her mind, and the other values self-restraint above all else. Laura is appalled by Susan's politics, and Susan is frankly judgmental of Laura's complacency and sense of superiority. "I work to get people green cards as a volunteer, while she sits on the board of a college," she says. "It's a huge disappointment not to be able to talk about politics with her and her husband—they're smart people—but I'm disappointed by their heartlessness." Still, she appreciates their authentic virtues: "My brother-in-law let a family live in his apartment and tried to save the man's business—he can be so generous. It's so inconsistent." In a situation like this, avoidance is the only strategy that, mostly, works.

Politics is not the only arena in which Laura expresses negative feelings without realizing it; she also told me that for many years her sister weighed twenty pounds more than she did and felt bad about it, although, "of course, I never brought it up." Susan acknowledges that she always felt competitive with Laura, who was "a brilliant student" who never had to study as hard as she did—as well as twenty pounds thinner. She also judges her sister for her "privileged" viewpoint, which, Susan believes, limits Laura's sensitivity to the plights of others. Their normal sibling rivalry was exacerbated by their family's focus on suppressing negative emotions when they were children, and it continues in their adult lives; they cannot ever address and make peace with the fact that they have opposing viewpoints.

Susan described an entirely different tone between her and her nephew, who is as staunch a conservative as his mother, Laura—another demonstration that character, not political conviction, determines whether or not people can discuss controversial issues amicably. Talking about contemporary politics is a pleasure for both of them. "He's willing to listen and hear my side of the story," Susan says. "He understands why I have my opinion even though he disagrees. I don't want to upset my nephew—we talk about his different perspective, and I respect it." Of course, it is easier to be open-minded with a nephew than a twin because there is less charged history to overcome.

The solution that aunt and nephew have discovered is based on sensitivity, respect, and mutual listening. If both parties feel heard, narcissistic injury, rage, and bitterness are reduced, and each side is more likely to see the other person as a human being with emotional needs and legitimate opinions, not just as a political adversary to be vanquished.

Being identical twins is no guarantee of political amity, any more than any other sibling relationship. Laura and Susan have their struggles, but their bond is probably the closest one in either of their lives, and they work to keep it that way to the best of their abilities. Both of them have independently concluded that avoiding ideological controversy is the best strategy, although it is not Susan's preference, but rather a reality she must accept to maintain a relationship that is central in her life. "Now when I go over there we talk about family and other things," Susan told me. "She's not a flexible person. We avoid raised voices, but it takes some effort. We're too mature to let it escalate again. We want to talk to each other, not just at each other." Laura adds, "As soon as we realize it's getting a little confrontational, we back off. We started to go down that path over the Trump agenda—but now if it starts to get heated we say, 'Let's change the subject.' I don't enjoy talking about politics." Their efforts are sincere and effective up to a point, even if not entirely satisfying to either of them.

They also make real mutual efforts to keep peace in the family by switching to nonincendiary topics of conversation to disperse any tension that builds. "She and I strategized about how to stay away from politics for the holidays," Susan said. "'How about those Mets?' we say." Luckily, most of their family roots for the same team, at least in baseball.

Susan added a striking observation about how central her sister is in her inner life, no matter how much they differ on politics: "She is always in my dreams because we're connected at the hip. Usually, she and I are going someplace together." Even if this recurrent dream is as much a wish as a reality, they both know they are, and will always be—and want to be—bound together. On this, they are in total agreement.

"If I could just plant little seeds": The Great Climate Change Debate

Ben and Jill Baker—he is a thirty-year-old photographer, she a thirty-three-year-old interior designer—have the deepest bond of any of the four siblings in their traditional Catholic, conservative Republican family. When Ben came out several years ago, Jill was the only one who empathized. "My family was out to dinner with friends. We have a gay member, and the way my parents were talking about it made me uncomfortable," she told me. In temperament and interests Ben and Jill have much in common, and this has not changed even as her politics has veered far to the left of his since she moved seven years ago from the family's hometown in Massachusetts to Washington. Both of them are determined not to let their closeness suffer because of the political and philosophical gap between them, and so they decided on a creative—if somewhat disingenuous—strategy to open a dialogue about climate change, a hot-button issue on which they have opposing views.

Jill was the one to propose the plan, and Ben concurred, although he was less sanguine, or perhaps more realistic, about its likelihood of success.

Jill suggested that they exchange partisan media reflecting each of their disparate points of view: She would send him a season of *Last Week Tonight with John Oliver* to watch, and he could send her something equivalent that she would read, watch, or listen to. Then they would discuss their reactions. "I told him, 'I'll open myself to your views if you tell me where to go to access them, what publications or media accurately represent them—whatever you think would resonate with me,'" she said. She also admitted a covert motive: "I always give him new information so he will end up having a deeper view of me, and I think over time he'll change his mind in my direction." Since Ben believed that no television or radio show accurately depicted his perspective, he sent her *A Climate of Crisis: America in the Age of Environmentalism,* a conservative book on the topic. They are now in the process of watching and reading at least some of what they gave each other, but have not had the discussion yet.

Ben felt less enthusiastic about the project than his sister did. He knew it would involve a commitment to spend a significant amount of time exposing himself to programs he had no interest in watching, and since they had already had a big fight on this topic that ended badly, he felt that neither of them was likely to change. Still, he was willing to try because it meant so much to Jill, and she meant so much to him.

Ben saw himself as having no illusions. "All people care about, including my sister, is fixing you, not listening to you," he said. "I know I can't budge my sister, and I don't try." Nonetheless, he hoped he might make a tiny dent in her liberalism if he approached her strategically. "You have to be willing to concede a piece of an issue—it helps create dialogue, makes the other person's mind a little bit open. When you don't give a heated rebuttal, they are more willing to hear." He plans to use this opportunity not so much to change his sister's mind as to reveal his to her in a less antagonistic light. "I sent that book to her to express my viewpoint," he explained. "Instead of attempting to change her, let's find topics where we can connect—we'll see if it works. She brought it up, and it could be a good thing. If I do what she asks, she promised that she'll listen to anything I want her to. This presents me with an opportunity to show her my own thoughts, to divorce myself from the current political status of the right wing, to let her see that it's not all groupthink."

"Why not tell her this directly?" I asked.

"She's incredibly stubborn and sensitive, so you need to give a little to have a conversation, whether you believe it or not," he admitted, frankly revealing his attempt at benign manipulation.

The siblings' private agendas were not entirely unrealistic. In recent years, Jill actually has changed her viewpoint on numerous issues, including religion (believer to atheist) and gay marriage (opponent to proponent), so she believes that Ben might do something equivalent. "My views have changed dramatically in the past few years, since I moved to the West Coast and was exposed to different points of view than I got from my family," she told me. "I realized I had been parroting what I heard around the dinner table and started to think for myself." Ben's beliefs, she hoped, might follow the same trajectory.

But there was a flaw in her argument: she had actively sought out different opinions and was internally receptive to changing her mind as part of developing her own identity and differentiating herself from her family and its politics. Ben felt no such need. Jill hopes to encourage him to consider other points of view as she has done, even though he is not as uncomfortable as she is hewing to the family's political line.

The odds that Ben and Jill will end up on the same page are not great, but this need not seriously damage their bond. Motives do not have to be pure in order to be legitimate, or to accomplish something, even if it is only goodwill.

At least neither one has grandiose hopes that his or her powers of persuasion will transform the other's views. "If I could just plant little seeds" was the way Jill described her plan. "I know I can't change my sister's mind, and I'm not going to try," Ben told me. What they both have in mind is subtle influence, not forcing their beliefs on the other, as was the case with many people I spoke to; there will be no PowerPoints or unsolicited article-thrustings. Both are willing participants, though with different degrees of optimism about the other's malleability. They both have complex motives, covert agendas—and respect for each other.

After I spoke separately to both siblings, it became clear to me that Jill is far more invested, emotionally as well as intellectually, in the outcome of the project; modifying her brother's heart and mind—even if ever so slightly—on something she considers so important means a great deal to her, because otherwise she will feel marooned in their family. She does not want to face life all alone in a sea of closed-minded conservatives without an ally. A powerful psychological need underlies her philosophical agenda, as is so often the case, and recognizing this would be enlightening for her.

Whatever the consequences, swapping partisan media as the basis for a political dialogue is a strategy that requires considerable goodwill to pull off. It asks a lot of the other person, and not every sibling—or spouse or friend—is willing to make such a commitment of time and energy. But the simple willingness to try it can cement an alliance, as long as expectations are limited and each participant knows when to stop pushing. Communication may improve, but deeply held convictions are unlikely to change, and both sides must be willing to accept that outcome.

If the project fails or backfires, it makes sense for them to face reality, call a truce, and focus more on the nonconflicted parts of their relationship as brother and sister—a bond that, luckily for them, will always be stronger than politics.

Where Did Our Childhood Love Go?

There was something poignant—almost desperate—in his response to my request for interview subjects who were embroiled in political disputes with people they loved: "My sister had a bitter fight with me. Not sure I want to open the scab with her," he began. Beneath the bitterness and bravado in Steve Nelson's terse offer lurked in the ruins of a rare childhood intimacy with his sister Sheila, which Steve, a sixty-four-year-old actuary, feared was lost forever, thanks to his own boorish behavior and right-wing rants. He longed for a way back to her—she is three years older and a left-leaning artists' agent—but had no idea what to do, and felt pessimistic that there was anything he could do; things had gotten so bad that occasional hostile emails were the only form of communication left between them.

Steve's MAGA diatribes exacerbated, but did not cause, their estrangement—nor was it the only one that he had provoked; both his older brother and his sister-in-law unfriended him on Facebook in response to his enraged and enraging posts and emails ("I was incredibly loathsome about Obama," he admitted). But since the 2016 election, political harangues have dominated his communications; he cannot think or talk about anything else. Now only his sister maintains any contact with him, even though his unceasing and entirely unsolicited efforts to force his politics down her throat severely strain their relationship. "She barely speaks to me since I voted for Trump and continue to defend him," he said, with resignation and regret. "Trump is everything." His ideological assaults and her offended responses are the only things left of their once-beloved companionship. What went awry, and is there any possibility of repair?

I asked Steve why he persisted in his obnoxious behavior when the outcome was so predictable.

"Why do you always go on the attack with your family?" I asked.

"I want them to know how I feel. I want them to know how wrong they are," he answered.

"Do you think you can change your brother's or your sister's mind?"

"Not effectively, no, but I want them to hear this."

"Why do you persist in something that's guaranteed to fail?"

"It's possible—I *thought* it's possible—to get through."

"When you come on so strong, the other person shuts down and gets defensive."

"But you have to put your cards on the table."

"What's the purpose of that?"

"Maybe nothing. I know I misspeak when I talk negatively like this, but we're political people."

"Is Trump really all you could write to them about?"

"We're all in little camps, aren't we?"

In this family, as in so many, a very old drama is being reenacted in the political realm. "Getting through," "showing them how I feel," "wanting them to hear this," and "putting my cards on the table" with his siblings are unmet needs from the past; contemporary politics is only the vehicle and justification for expressing them. Steve fails to see his own desire to make meaningful contact with his siblings and his desperation that he does not know how. He does not realize that he feels alone and unheard in his family—that he must have always felt this—and that his anger makes him try to force them to heed him in a manner that only makes them turn away. His right-wing politics is the weapon he had been looking for to cudgel them with, so he cannot give it up. For others in his predicament, left-wing politics would work just as well.

Since Steve expressed regret that he had already alienated his brother, I wondered why he was continuing to risk losing Sheila as well. He gave me several explanations that did not really explain it: Their lives had diverged. He was much better off financially, and "way, way down" he felt she envied his prosperity. He was a conservative Catholic, and she was unconventional and irreligious and had liberal values and liberal friends. The most painful—and telling—thing he said was, "I think she thinks I've gone the wrong way in life in a way I don't think about her."

I was not at all sure that this was true, rather than simply a projection of his own fears about himself. He had been carrying a chip on his shoulder for a very long time.

But his tone changed radically, from bitterness to tenderness, when I asked Steve about his and Sheila's closeness as children.

"What do you appreciate about her?" I wondered. His answer surprised and moved me: "I feel a deep connection with her. She lives the life of the mind and values truth and beauty."

I was so affected by this loving and discerning—and completely unexpected—response that I revealed something painful about my own life in the hope that he could make use of it: "If my brother had ever said something so appreciative and understanding of me, I would have felt truly known by him. I'd be willing to overlook political differences, and probably lots of other things. You should tell her this."

"The problem is that Trump is everything," he repeated, from the automaton part of himself. He did not feel vulnerable as long as he was on the attack.

"But you just contradicted that—it's not true," I insisted. "The way you talk about this relationship shows that it is precious to you even though you two have major disagreements. You can take active steps to keep your convictions from destroying your love for each other." His sincerity convinced me that if he expressed his genuine feelings and controlled his need to lash out, this relationship could be saved.

The most important thing Steve needs to do with Sheila is to communicate directly with her. He has to shut off his computer and pick up the phone, or arrange to meet her in person. What he has to say is too important to risk its being dismissed or misinterpreted by playing it safe and keeping his feelings at arm's length.

Then Steve began reminiscing about their shared childhood. "We were both academically successful," he said. "When we were small, we played 'dog' together"—a game so private that he could not explain it to me. "Later we talked about our romances."

I felt he was lonely for her companionship and did not know how to talk about his longing or his true feelings, which are deep and appreciative under his obnoxious, alienating veneer. "If you must have a political discussion," I suggested, "preface it by saying, 'Here's my point of view, even though I know you disagree. I want to hear and understand yours.'"

What made me optimistic is that Steve took responsibility for setting the tone of these exchanges, and seemed genuinely sorry that he had alienated both of his siblings, but especially Sheila. "I've been too divisive and allowed this to happen," he admitted. "I have to deal differently with this relationship I care about."

Maybe Trump was not everything, after all.

When I wrote to Steve several months after our conversation and asked if things had improved between him and Sheila, I got a response that was just as succinct as his initial communication but quite different in tone: "Pretty much, yes. We just avoid politics." That "just" took a lot of work, and I was impressed that he had done it.

⁂

"All I want is to be seen, heard, and appreciated for who I am" was the sentiment I heard expressed sorrowfully, and often passionately, by every politically divergent son and daughter confronting intransigent parents, whether the adult children tried repeatedly to explain their points of view, or simply longed for their parents to understand and accept the legitimacy of their stance but had no idea how to communicate this universal desire—sentiments and struggles that siblings feel about each other as well. Sometimes, of course, they did not voice their need directly because they knew what the outcome would be and wanted to avoid a complete breakdown of relations; I was touched and saddened by how much children of all ages struggled to get through to their parents, and retain a bond with them, even when the parents behaved badly. Parents were as much in the dark about how to do this as their offspring were.

There were also instances, sometimes not acknowledged

by the child, of trying to change a parent's mind; this was especially true of daughters with their mothers. Of course, this goal is just as hopeless in families as it is in marriages and friendships. Recognizing this can help people try the far more effective strategy of communicating without a hidden agenda.

With one impressive exception, the mothers and fathers of my interview subjects, and the parents I interviewed, expected allegiance and deference from their sons and daughters, no matter how old their children were. Parents want to see their own reflections in their children, and this is natural; problems arise when parents feel outraged and betrayed by differences and interpret them as repudiations. Shared politics is far from the only way the generations can be connected—and, as my subjects learned, even age and illness can often be overcome.

Political accord, an elusive goal in families because of built-in generational tensions, and between siblings because of ancient rivalries, has taken on more urgency lately. Now it often represents a last-ditch effort to achieve connection and agreement in at least one arena—a difficult goal in many family relationships. Siblings who disagree have the same struggles, the same longings, and often the same difficulty communicating their hope for a resolution they can live with as parents and children do; they don't want to lose each other, but don't know how to keep each other.

Conflicts over ideology have a way of blinding people to other, more fundamental things they have in common. Simply acknowledging their longing, and reminding themselves and each other of what is good in their relationship, would go a long way toward helping them find a way to live with their political differences. Many family stories can have a new chapter when both partners reach out.

5

Relentless Hope

The Dangerous Delusion That We Can Change Another Person's Politics

There is a pernicious assumption that transcends party lines, ideology, gender, and age. It is responsible for the most bitter, persistent, and interminable fights—the kind that destroy relationships with people who love each other. This is the unshakable conviction that it is not only possible but imperative to change another person's political opinions. People on both sides of the aisle are convinced that they can do this, if only they are persuasive and persistent enough. The same compulsion embroils us in hopeless love affairs—something that 98 percent of the population has experienced.[†] Political persuasion is our national bad love affair.

---

† R. Baumeister, S. Wotman, and A. Stillwell, "Unrequited Love: On

People do change their minds about politics and many other things, but never because we make them do so. Yet we cling to this goal and pursue it unceasingly—even desperately.

Why does the fantasy that we have this superhuman power continue to seduce us? The compulsive need to convert clouds our judgment because the alternative feels unbearable, particularly in the contemporary world, where politics has become so central to identity that not sharing ideology with an intimate partner seems inconceivable to most people. If someone we love votes differently than us, we have to do something about it, or we feel left alone. We can't win, but we refuse to give up; human nature makes it so.

An enormous amount of energy is wasted in this tragic pursuit, yet this travesty of authentic hope (the psychoanalytic term for it is "relentless hope"[††]) springs eternal, sowing grief, rage, bitterness, and despair—without ever effecting the ideological transformation we long for and believe we can and must bring about in another person's heart and mind. It is an unshakable conviction, and a task many people are devoting themselves to—with disastrous results.

Heartbreak, Anger, Guild, Scriptlessness, and Humiliation," *Journal of Personality and Social Psychology* 64, no. 3 (March 1993): 377–94.
[††] Martha Stark, M.D., *Relentless Hope: The Refusal to Grieve* (International Psychotherapy Institute, 2017), ebook. Dr. Stark originated this evocative term.

"Why is politics so important to me that I feel I have to risk this relationship?"

The doomed pursuit of political proselytizing is virtually a religious calling for Wendy Jenkins, a thirty-eight-year-old teacher. Showing her mother-in-law, an enthusiastic Trump supporter, the error of her ways is Wendy's mission in life, at whatever cost. She clings to it as a guiding principle despite her complete lack of success and the painful awareness that she has already damaged a relationship she cherishes, one she knows is irreplaceable.

There were rumblings of discontent about her mother-in-law's conservatism—Wendy is an ardent liberal, as well as a serious Quaker—in the twenty years they have known each other, but before the 2016 election she managed to restrain herself and, mostly, avoid the topic. Wendy readily admits that her mother-in-law is a wonderful woman; indeed, she is more maternal, loving, and giving than her own mother, who shares her daughter's politics. Not only are Wendy and her mother-in-law very close—only ideology divides them—but the elder Mrs. Jenkins takes daily care of her grandchildren, whom she adores and who adore her.

Wendy's outrage at Trump and his policies, and her devastation at her mother-in-law's support for both, have made her obsessed with changing the other woman's mind, despite receiving no support from her husband and many exhortations to cease and desist from her friends. "Pretty much no one thinks I'm justified or doing any good in bringing up the subject with her," she admitted—yet she persists, ostensibly on moral grounds. She feels she must speak up. "I can't maintain the polite silence on politics that we've had since forever anymore," she said. "I've said to more than one friend, 'I need a support group for people who are still trying to talk to their family about politics!'"—by which she means foisting her opinions on an unwilling audience. Alas, the group she and those like her really need, Political Proselytizers Anonymous, doesn't yet exist. I imagine her qualifying by saying, "I'm Wendy, and I can't stop trying to convert my mother-in-law."

It doesn't help that Wendy's mother-in-law wants to avoid conflict about this issue at all costs and keeps her opinions to herself, trying to evade the debate her daughter-in-law constantly presses upon her. This makes Wendy's job of converting her considerably more risky and frustrating; Wendy insists she just wants to "get through," to explain her own positions, and to understand why her mother-in-law has the opinions she has, but the pained and angry reactions she gets indicate that her agenda is far more intrusive and confrontational than she admits. Everything boiled over in a "discussion" in front of her ten-year-old son: "I asked her how she was feeling after Trump's election, and she said, 'I'm feeling calmer.' I instantly felt adrenalinized. We talked for an hour and a half, and my son got upset because we were speaking louder and more force-fully than normal. So now I text her even though I know it's not the best way."

On another occasion Wendy felt compelled to inform the other woman that her sister's insurance premiums "went sky-high under Trump," then took offense when she was told, "I don't want to talk about it." She cannot take no for an answer. "I acquiesce to her requirements, but I also feel myself withholding myself from her and disliking her," she admitted. Not engaging about these issues is, for Wendy, a blot on the elder Mrs. Jenkins's character that nothing else she does, and all the love she gives, can remove.

Limitations in their communication, or gaps in their rapport, feel intolerable to Wendy. Intimacy, virtue, and political like-mindedness are inextricably linked in her mind, and it torments her that she cannot have it all with a woman she admires and relies upon, literally and emotionally. Her own mother, Wendy frankly admitted, "is completely in tune with me politically, but has never been helpful in my life, while my mother-in-law has been there, hands on." With an encouraging glimmer of insight, she added, "Why is politics so important to me that I feel I have to risk this relationship?"

Relentless hope has her in its spell. "I take her views personally, as lack of respect for me," she explained—and significantly, this conviction changed not at all when she actually succeeded in convincing the older woman to vote for a Democratic candidate running for a statewide office. It was a Pyrrhic victory, because the discrepancy in their convictions was still glaring. "It didn't make me feel as much better as I hoped it would," she acknowledged, "because anything she does isn't enough."

Total political mind-meld is the only acceptable solution. "It's a worldview thing," she said. "Trump is destroying the values that matter most to me. I'm trying to give her a chance to have a deeper relationship," which for Wendy can only mean acquiescing to a full political makeover. And she genuinely believes that she might be able to bring this about. "People close to me think I'm nuts, but I don't feel it's hopeless; if every person in America tried really hard to reach an understanding with somebody who voted for Trump, we'd be a step further along from where we are," she insisted. I have my doubts about the likely success of this enterprise, especially if all those Trump supporters pursued the same agenda with their opponents. The competing crusades that would ensue would leave us exactly where we are—battered and even more bitterly disappointed.

Wendy cannot bear that she and her maternal surrogate will never see eye to eye politically, because it means that she will never have the ideal mother she longs for; it is at root a psychological problem, not an ideological one. She cannot stand to know that there is nothing whatever she can do to make her mother-in-law agree with her, because the other woman is a separate person with her own ideas. Wendy has not dealt with the depth of her disappointment with her politically correct but emotionally limited biological mother, so she is trying to create a better model by attempting to alter her mother-in-law's politics by friendly persuasion, and risking a breach in the process. This is particularly tragic because the two women genuinely love each other.

No one has the power to unilaterally change the mind or the heart of another person. To avoid this sobering conclusion, people make endless efforts that never work, always hoping for the impossible and protecting themselves from the truth.

Wendy's problem—and America's problem in these fraught times—is a striking example of the tenacity of relentless hope. The failure to grieve for past disappointments and to acknowledge the limits of one's power over other people perpetuates the cycle, in love and in politics. The same compulsion that keeps us seeking blood from a stone in impossible romantic relationships with unresponsive partners causes us to persist in the futile pursuit of perfect political harmony, driving us never to give up trying to impose our opinions on people we can never persuade, and jeopardizing precious bonds in the process. It feels unbearable to face the fact that political differences are here to stay. This dynamic is what motivates the devastating political fights that are tearing apart relationships like Wendy's with her mother-in-law.

The identical impulse drives us to try to force people to love us and to agree with us. Both efforts are doomed to fail and leave serious damage in their wake. But, in fact, accepting political differences is a much more realistic enterprise than pursuing unresponsive lovers; you actually can have an intimate bond with somebody who votes for the other party—and even if you vote identically, there will always be significant areas of disagreement over which you have no control. Limitations in close relationships, including radical differences of opinion about things that matter, in politics and many other arenas, are a fact of life—a fact of life we can live with.

Relentless hope is a perversion of authentic hope. We cling to it and pursue it at all costs in order to avoid feeling the pain of disappointment in the other person, who, despite our efforts, refuses to change. Pursuing a conversion agenda prevents us from ever seeing that this is an impossible task, and from feeling the full brunt of the recognition of just how limited our sway over other people actually is. Forced political makeovers are no more successful than unilateral romantic makeovers.

Ultimately, the problem is not how we vote or which side we support, and the solution does not involve acquiring the debating skills necessary to make arguments compelling enough to convert or crush an intimate opponent. The real issue is our mistaken belief that intimacy is only possible with people who agree with us on everything. This stubborn conviction represents a profound distortion of the essence of love, the hidden fundamentals of human relationships and their discontents, and the nature of hope.

In our increasingly narcissistic world, the other person is but an extension of ourselves politically as well as emotionally—when in fact it is only by accepting and appreciating our very real differences that true intimacy becomes possible. Otherwise we are just trying to see our own reflections.

We cannot bear feeling that we are unable to impose our will, or that the success of our efforts of persuasion, whether in love or politics, is minimal. To do so requires us to accept powerlessness, disappointment, and loneliness—the unavoidable consequences of recognizing the fundamental otherness of an intimate partner. The sobering, but ultimately liberating, truth is that nobody will ever fully understand or accept the world exactly as we see it—and nobody has to. Forgoing relentless hope allows authentic hope—for communication, dialogue, appreciation of another person's qualities—to flourish. It underlies precious, loving mixed-political relationships.

How can Wendy get out of her predicament? She has to change her relationship to the differences that exist between herself and her mother-in-law, and accept that they are immutable but not catastrophic. In a case like this, what she has to change is her *relationship to the disagreement* itself. Wendy needs to see her mother-in-law's opinions in the context of her personality and her value system, and recognize that these can never be identical to her own because the two women have different histories. Her mother-in-law, like every intimate political opponent, is a fundamentally separate entity. Accepting this would restore the trust that Wendy's messianic zeal has eroded.

Political diversity is only one of many manifestations of the fact that your partner is an independent person with a unique set of ideas and emotions, as entrenched and immutable as your own. Differences of every sort are here to stay; to insist that these must change is to court disaster. Fortunately for us, lockstep agreement is not only not possible, it is not necessary. Authentic communication becomes a reality only when you give up trying to change your partner, realize the limitations of even the closest relationship, appreciate the unique qualities of the other, recognize your own contribution to the controversy, and welcome the other person's efforts to meet you halfway. The result of this challenging project is lasting love and mutual appreciation to a degree that few couples—spouses, relatives, in-laws, or friends—who start out agreeing ever achieve.

6

Enemies No Longer

Advice from Couples Who Have Stopped Fighting about Politics

It is a common assumption that intimate relationships between partners who have major political disagreements are doomed; who wants to battle all the time, or suppress passionately held convictions? How can love and empathy flourish in an atmosphere of tension, when you revile the principles your mate holds dear? Most people cannot imagine that there could ever be peace and joy in such a bond, and that they would not feel lonely or angry, or both, all the time.

This assumption is wrong.

Nobody has to settle for political misery at home. With effort, self-awareness, and tact, many bipartisan couples really do figure out how to revere each other despite serious differences of opinion that they refuse to allow to become deal-breakers. This usually happens after a few hard knocks along the way, as was the case with my husband and me. It takes work and goodwill—what relationship does not?

In every case, couples I spoke to—spouses, lovers, and close friends who have found a way to live with major ideological dissonance—believe that their bonds are stronger and more resilient because they figured out how to deal with their different takes on many critical issues. They had no argument about the fundamental values they shared, which were their abiding love, respect, and delight in each other. On this they were in complete agreement.

The process they went through, and continue to go through, shows that it can be done, it should be done, and people of goodwill can figure out a way to do it. The chasm that separates them turns out to be less perilous than they feared.

"I love my husband more than I love my country"

Election Night 2016 at Carlos* and Nancy's* New York City apartment was not a fun place to be. This couple, forty-seven and forty-one, respectively—he is a restaurateur, she a real estate agent—who had been married for five years and together for eight, had voted for different candidates. Their diametrically opposed reactions to Trump's unex-

pected triumph could have endangered their otherwise
excellent relationship. "I was really upset," Nancy, a fervent
liberal and a feminist, recalled. "My reaction was so raw—
all of a sudden it was like one of the sexist men I used to
work with had become president, and I couldn't stop crying. I felt unsafe and unprotected. Carlos told me to stop
crying, and that made me even more upset."

"I feel helpless when she cries, like I'm supposed to fix
it and I can't—like it was with my mother," Carlos explained. "I felt awful that she thought I'd betrayed her by
putting a man like that in power, but I felt justified in voting for Trump. I couldn't vote for a woman who enabled
her husband the way Hillary did. This was the first time
ever that the candidate I voted for won, so I got defensive."
His frank and insightful explanation, and his empathy
with the way she felt despite their differences of opinion
about the outcome, made Nancy feel somewhat better ("I
understand why he gets worked up when I cry," she said),
although she was still miserable.

They came from different worlds. Nancy is from an old-
stock Yankee family who arrived in America in 1630,
and Carlos describes himself as "a first-generation Latino
Republican, a rare breed, the only one I know." Usually
Nancy is both proud and protective of him ("He's mine—I
never want to hear my friends talk down to him. They have
a sense of privilege they're not aware of, and they would
never be able to put themselves in his shoes," she said), but

on Election Night she felt inconsolable. An emotional gulf she had never noticed before now seemed to yawn between them.

The pain and the tension they both felt that night were sobering, and made them realize that their marriage would be in jeopardy if they did not figure out how to deal with politics. So they talked it out, and the decision they made has served them well ever since: judicious silence.

"We agree about maybe 40 percent of the issues. The rest we don't talk about anymore," Nancy said. "Carlos would continue to discuss everything, but I put the kybosh on that, because if we engage with each other in this way it's not going to be good for our relationship. It's an imperative. I love my husband more than I love my country, so we had to figure out how to get through this."

"We talked about it in depth that one time, and noticed how we both got worked up, so we stopped," said Carlos, more succinctly but just as passionately. "Love for each other comes first."

What makes it possible for them to abide by the principle of intentional avoidance of conflict is the depth of their appreciation for each other's efforts, even in the face of major disagreements; love comes first, politics a distant second. Nancy saw proof of this not long after that traumatic Election Night when she announced the following January that she was going on the Women's March in Washington, DC, on the day after Trump's inauguration to protest his election. Despite how he had voted, Carlos backed her up wholeheartedly. "He was very supportive when I went," she said. "He made sure I had warm clothes, food, and drink, and saw me off at three a.m."

Actions count, and his were tender and true.

"We gave up trying to convert each other"

You would think that a couple who have as much in common as Daniel and Karen Schwartz would be in sync ideologically as well. Married six years and together for eight, they jointly run a used-book business and share a serious interest in current events. They are also both evangelical Christians who belong to the same church and consider their faith the cornerstone of their lives. However, their interpretations of this faith are diametrically opposed: he thinks their church is too liberal; she considers it too conservative. When a couple believe that politics mirrors religious convictions, the situation can be incendiary if their principles clash. But the opposite has happened: they started out with missionary zeal to change each other's views—with predictably negative results—and have since made concerted efforts to understand and alter the dynamic between them instead, with impressive success.

In the early days of their relationship, they were virtually at each other's throats about every controversial issue. Their verbal skirmishes generated so much tension that they decided to avoid discussing politics at all. "For the first three years, we couldn't bring up anything in the news without raising our voices and lecturing each other," Karen told me, "and sometimes we still slip up. Now, though, not a week goes by in which we don't talk about something controversial, and it's often three or more times a week." She is usually the one to initiate a topic, which, thanks to their joint exertions, mostly leads to a conversation rather than a conflict.

What changed? For Karen, it was a combination of self-control, experience, and a growing appreciation of her husband's character that ultimately transcended their serious differences of opinion. "I've come to recognize and trust that he doesn't consider other people inferior, and I'm no longer afraid that he doesn't care about human suffering," she said. As a result, she frames what she says differently. "I think my questions for Daniel have become less antagonistic—less 'How can you possibly believe that?' and more 'Do you think [something I heard on NPR] is a fair assessment of why conservatives don't like [this policy]?' And I've learned to listen more than to talk. Now I tend to catch myself before I say, 'How dare you think that!'" Karen's feistiness and the intensity of her convictions are unaltered, but her presentation is considerably more subtle and less combative than it used to be.

She credits both of their efforts for the relative tranquility and maturity of their current exchanges, even on hot-button issues like immigration, which is still difficult for them to discuss calmly. The Schwartzes have discovered that tone and attitude count—and that relinquishing relentless hope counts most of all. "The most important change we've made," as Karen put it, "is that we've both given up the hope of trying to convert the other and focus on trying to understand instead. Now I say, 'Does this make sense to you?' instead of thinking, 'If only I could come up with the right article to make him see the light!'"

Their changes in attitude have had positive effects beyond politics—a perk that many mixed couples have discovered and profited from. "I'm less sensitive and he is less rigid—he used to have to verify the claims he made by always showing me a study, and he seemed put out that I didn't listen to him," Karen said. "Now he knows that I don't think he's uninterested or making stuff up." No more article-thrusting for either one of them.

Living together has taught them to trust one another, even when they are on opposite sides of an issue. "We had to grow comfortable enough in our relationship and in our respect for each other as intelligent, decent individuals before we could hear views we found offensive without having them change our opinions of one another. We've seen enough evidence that the other person was worthy of regard, even if they were obviously wrong on a particular issue." Fights automatically become less acrid when you admire your opponent.

Giving up trying to win arguments turned out to be as important as renouncing the conversion imperative. Now it no longer matters, and no longer threatens their bond, that they do not agree any more than they ever did. As I know from my own marriage, this is a comforting experience.

Their mutual values count the most. "Our shared religious beliefs are more important than our political views," Karen said. "This gives us some apolitical common ground—even though we disagree pretty strongly about which political side aligns most closely with them."

Karen's admiration for her husband has even changed her view of his political party; she altered her attitude toward Republicans in general based on her high opinion of the one she is married to—a rare thing indeed. "At the beginning, a relationship with a conservative Republican was not something I felt was very likely for me—some people could never imagine it," she said. "Before I met Daniel, talking about how evil and stupid Republicans are was a way of group bonding, and only after I had a relationship with an actual Republican did it bother me. Now I find I get into vociferous arguments with people who say all Republicans are evil and stupid." She also told me that their joint opposition to Trump has finally given them something political to agree about without reservation, a delicious respite for any liberal married to a non-Trump conservative.

Another one of the Schwartzes' discoveries is that decibels matter. This is much more important than most people realize, and can prevent accelerations of ill will in many an argument, but it requires self-awareness. "Whenever we used to discuss politics, it escalated into us talking louder and louder and interrupting each other," Karen said. "It reminds me of how I fought with my younger brother when I was four." People usually consider themselves entirely rational, which is never the whole truth; identifying the irrational childhood origins of adult conflicts helps put them into perspective and can even inject some refreshing humor into the proceedings.

Daniel echoed many of his wife's observations. "We've grown together," he said. "We've become confident enough that we don't need to change each other's mind. We trust one another. People think that political agreement is more important than it really is in a relationship"—quite a statement from a man for whom politics is such a central concern. He, too, does not minimize the intensity of their disagreements and the powerful emotions they still evoke, which makes their achievement even more impressive.

"Here's our method: we've learned more about ourselves. For example, we both have a tendency to raise our voices, which is interpreted by the other as shouting. When we really think and tone it down, we are able not to get angry. At first, when she took a hard-line position, it led me to take a hard-line position. We've gotten better at not doing this. One of the things that made a difference was to assume good faith. You can get on the internet and see an issue and think, 'How could the other side possibly believe this thing?'—but if you tone your comments down and you are willing to listen to the way you make them, it helps you see the other side of the issue more objectively."

Assuming good faith was a common denominator in every mixed-political relationship I saw that worked, and it usually took time to accomplish.

I wondered whether there was anything they still could not discuss amicably, even with all the work they had done. Without hesitation, Daniel said, "Immigration. We draw the line at different places. It's possible to believe something is wrong without thinking it should be illegal—and mercy is an important consideration in this case—but I believe strongly that national sovereignty is paramount." His positions are nuanced and deeply considered, and I could see why Karen came to appreciate his thoughtfulness despite her adamant opposition to his conclusions.

Daniel admits that they still have to work at discretion and self-control, as every mixed couple—and every other couple—must. "I appreciate what we've learned, mostly about acting calmly and listening; it works. You're always tempted to interrupt and say, 'That's wrong'—and you have to try not to do that."

The most important indicator of what the Schwartzes have accomplished is that they sound remarkably similar when they talk about how their fights and their feelings have evolved. They have dramatically altered the way they interact about differences of opinion that can and do tear many marriages apart. Their stances on those issues have not budged, but their love has deepened as a result.

"Politics isn't a religion; it's not more important than love or family"

She came from a lineage so devoutly Republican that when an appliance broke in her home when she was a child, somebody always said, "It went Democratic on me." He is a centrist (and sometime Obama voter) who believes that partisan politics like hers is the bane of America, a threat to the democratic process, and a dangerously polarizing force that he works to combat. Their contrary opinions of Sarah Palin, Republican John McCain's choice as his running mate in 2008, almost derailed their engagement plans. These days, they disagree professionally on CNN and are still at serious odds about most political issues in private. And yet their delight in each other's company and intellect after nine years of marriage is a joy to behold. Margaret Hoover* and John Avlon,* both political animals, have achieved what many people find inconceivable: their opposing views have done no serious damage to their relationship. How is this possible?

Margaret, forty-one, is a political commentator on CNN and host on PBS of a new edition of William F. Buckley Jr.'s interview program *Firing Line*. She comes by her anti-Democratic, passionately committed Republicanism legitimately: she is a great-granddaughter of President Herbert Hoover, whom Franklin D. Roosevelt and the Democrats blamed personally for the Great Depression. "He was the most vilified president of the twentieth century," she said, and her family has never forgiven or forgotten this. So deep are the intergenerational wounds in the Hoover family that Margaret is the first of them to refer to the former East River Drive in New York City, officially renamed for Roosevelt after his death, as "the FDR Drive."

Margaret and John met as colleagues on Rudy Giuliani's presidential campaign in 2008. When Margaret first came for an interview, John was already working as Giuliani's speechwriter and director of policy; a prescient friend announced to him, "I just met the girl you're going to marry," before they were even introduced. Margaret was immediately intrigued with John, despite his unorthodox (i.e., not doctrinaire Republican) political views.

Their attraction was complicated from the start.

John, the forty-six-year-old third-generation descendant of Greek immigrants, is a CNN anchor and a political independent who appreciates why his relationship with Margaret had such a rocky beginning, and how far they have come. "In her family, politics is absolutely a religion," he said. "The fact that I wasn't a Republican meant she would be marrying outside the faith. Tribalism is hard-wired in her."

Margaret agrees with his assessment. "When I met John I was pretty severely ideological, and it really was tribal for me. The Hoovers lived with a social stigma. The effect on family psychology was to put everyone into a defensive crouch. My grandfather was depressed all the time, and I took on his political philosophy. Nobody in my family had ever voted or married outside the party. Being a Republican was my religion. This has changed since we married; things had to change to make it work. I've grown as a result of our relationship."

Just as Margaret became the defender of the family's political orthodoxy, John's political identity as a man in the middle was also based on his childhood experience—in his case, his self-appointed role as the family peacemaker. "I was the eldest kid," he told me. "My parents fought but never got divorced. I couldn't fall asleep if I heard them fighting; I would get out of bed and try to mediate. I'd say, 'Can't we get along?'" He now advocates the same approach for the country at large.

John's well-honed skills as a reconciler came in handy in the most important negotiation of his life: winning over the woman for whom anybody who did not vote the straight Republican ticket was outside the pale.

Their marriage almost didn't happen because of politics. John had already bought the ring when McCain picked Sarah Palin, the inexperienced first-term governor of Alaska and a divisive figure, for his running mate. When John announced to Margaret that this choice was so unacceptable to him that he was going to vote for Obama instead, she almost called the whole thing off.

"I was planning to propose, and she said she didn't know if she could marry someone who thought Sarah Palin was a birdbrain—for her it was 'the team.' We had a really big fight, and it caused a crisis of faith in our relationship," John recalled.

Using skills he had learned as a boy, John tried to employ humor to deflect his beloved's outrage, but she was adamant. "She really wondered whether we should stay together," he said. Deeply held core values were on the line.

Finally they came to a resolution. As John put it, "We realized that Sarah Palin isn't something we want to fight and die over." "It took a very long time," Margaret explained, "before I could assume best intentions. You have to believe that the person you love isn't coming to the fight with knives. I had a series of incredible experiences with John, and it didn't feel like I was undermining my family history."

Ultimately, Margaret got out of her defensive crouch and walked down the aisle with her nonbeliever. "I recognized that he was the person I knew I wanted to marry, who appreciated me and my family history independent of any label—it felt like a risk, it really did. But I felt like the downside of not taking this risk was that I would lose the best man I ever met. I felt I could take the leap of faith."

What finally saved the day was their mutual realization that "the Sarah Palin Fight"—they still laughingly refer to the crisis that way—really had little to do with the notorious vice-presidential candidate. John said, "It was not about Sarah Palin—she was only the trigger. It was really about whether I was rejecting Margaret and her family and her identity. This was the serious debate below the absurdity of the occasion." He understood the real issues and took them to heart. When they both grasped what was really going on, they realized that their union would not endanger the values of either one of them. Then they could see that what seemed like impediments to their marriage of true minds was not a real threat. Insight conquered all.

Now, after nine years of marriage and two children, they have not overcome their differences—that would be both impossible and unnecessary—but they have put them in perspective. "We still have deep divides in personal style as well as principles," John said. "Even though I'm not naturally patient, outreach to one another takes work and perseverance."

"Outreach" to a partner who disagrees with you is not

something many couples think of. It involves conveying that you take the other person's radically different attitudes and beliefs seriously, that you respect their validity, and that you will listen to them with an open mind, just as you want to be listened to; attempts at conversion are not an option in a union that works.

But Margaret and John also have to navigate their differences in public, in front of a television audience. John in particular has modified his stance in both the private and public arenas considerably since his marriage. "I genuinely enjoy debating—the object is to win. But this does not translate into marriage, where I've learned not to try to win. Politics isn't a religion; it's not more important than love or family. You can't demonize or disrespect in personal life, or feel the need to win every argument definitively." This is quite a statement coming from a professional debater, and a strategy that other couples would do well to try at home. He has developed a technique for defusing arguments in private life: "If I'm getting my blood up, I need to remember I'm debating with my wife, not with a friend or colleague—I shouldn't push. It's a muscle you develop, and it's rooted in love. That's more important than winning any debate. The personal transcends all of it."

The couple also consciously tries to present an alternative model in their on-air personas. "We're both on CNN, with our different perspectives—our political philosophies are still opposite," John acknowledged; divergent positions on health care is but one ongoing hot-button example. And their mutual opposition to Trump is a rare point of agreement. "She's still a proud partisan, and I still think that's a problem, but we symbolize a hopeful trend, that you can disagree agreeably." Underlying John's discretion is his sensitivity to Margaret's heritage; "I remember that my children are also Hoover's great-great-grandchildren."

I wondered if John ever defended his wife publicly from attackers who agreed with him. He responded, "On social media, my impulse is 'That's my wife. Back off—don't you demonize the woman I love.'" I had no doubt that she would do the same if the situation were reversed. This is absolutely essential in a union like theirs.

"The reason people respond to us when we're on the air together is that it shows it's possible to get over disagreements," John said. Margaret added, "I like John's phrase 'Check your ideology at the door.' He's principled. Before I met him I used to love people based on their politics. John helped me learn it's more important to be attached to people because you love them rather than because of the way they vote. I changed because I recognized I could still be me. The thing that's most important in our lives is our relationships."

And that's something that will NEVER go Democratic on you.

"I love a good debate"

What are Harry,* a sixty-six-year-old advertising copy-writer, and Allan,* a seventy-seven-year-old retired soft-ware engineer, doing in this chapter? Combative to the core, they seem on the face of it to be the polar opposite of the other couples, who have toned things down over time and learned to avoid or deflect controversy. These two men have not only not stopped fighting about politics in the decades they have been dear friends, they have honed it into an art form—a game, a sport, and a dance that is a delight, and an education, to behold. They are the senior poster children for passionate but sane political disputa-tion.

None of their opinions, which are well considered and thoughtfully expressed, have changed one iota over time, although they have refined and ritualized their arguments in support of these opinions. Their friendship is stronger than ever, and their political battles are an integral part of it. They demonstrate that it truly is possible to agree about nothing political, talk about opposing views incessantly, and grow ever closer over time. Their secret weapon is emo-tional management, coupled with discretion, humor, and a policy of avoiding grudges.

Over the years their debates have evolved into a rou-tine. A weekly dinner and a drink or two set the stage for the centerpiece of these evenings: a serious ideological argument, usually provoked by the headlines but wide-ranging—always both emotional and partisan, but civil and devoid of bitterness. The combatants don't usually have an agenda of topics in advance, but they know the drill after decades of practice as well as they know each other's stance on the issues. These good-natured, opinionated sparring partners have a ritual honed over a very long time and through numerous life experiences and administrations, both Democratic and Republican.

They met when both men were habitués of a local bar in the Manhattan neighborhood where they lived. "I honestly don't know how the politics thing started," Harry said. "One of us must have reacted to something in the news, and the other one piped up, putting the other in his place, and that was that." Even after Harry moved out of the neighborhood, they continued the habit with dinners at each other's homes. For two decades, they were family and couple friends, and eventually they helped each other through the devastation of each man's spouse's sudden death.

There is something comical, as well as serious and intellectually stimulating, about their set-tos. Allan is much taller, his speech is more deliberate and often ironic, and his sense of humor is bone dry. Harry is shorter, feistier, and more provocative as a combatant. Watching them argue is like seeing a small dog mixing it up with a large dog; each has his strengths as a debater, so definitive victories are rare.

"It's a game we play," said Allan. "He's a good debater. We both like intellectual games, and it's hard to find a good adversary." "It helps when you have facts on your side," Harry responds, a little mockingly. "Mainly from Fox News, in your case," Allan retorts, teasing him back. "Is irony and humor part of what makes this work?" I ask. "Definitely!" they both say at once. "It's only politics, it's just an election," adds Harry. Then Allan gets more serious for a moment: "But that's what Jews were saying in 1932." "But this isn't Germany—checks and balances work here," Harry insists. They are so evenly matched that neither one ever really gets the upper hand for very long.

How do they manage to spar so constantly, without things ever getting out of hand? Allan said, "The rule of a good debater is never lose your temper." "Where did you learn that?" I asked. "I don't know," he said. "It just comes naturally. Otherwise you're not debating—you're just yelling. You have to talk politely."

I also asked whether Trump's election had changed the tenor of their contests.

ALLAN: Well, from my point of view, it's a whole different story since Trump came on board. For the first time I think that maybe our democracy is in some danger because of him—I never thought that about any previous Republican president.

HARRY: Oh good heavens! I mean, our democracy is

not in any danger. If our democracy was in danger at all from Russian collusion, go say hi to Hillary, who probably benefited more from that.

ALLAN: Harry, how can you make a silly statement like that when everybody—FBI, CIA—says that the goal of Russian intervention was to sow discord by aiding Donald Trump, knowing full well that Trump is the master of discord?

[They then talked over each other unintelligibly.]

The only time things truly got vicious was once when an uninvited third party overheard them at the bar and commented. "Sometimes other people join in," said Harry. "We were arguing about global warming—which of course is a joke—and somebody in the bar says to me, 'I hope your children die horrible deaths!'"

I wanted to know how Allan—who radically disagrees with Harry's position on the issue—reacted to this.

"I like his children. I don't want them to die—I want *him* to die," he said with a twinkle in his eye.

I noticed that Harry wasn't offended in the least. "We laugh a lot," he said, since he could give as good as he got. Here was an example of expressing hostility in an absurdly over-the-top form, which delighted them both—a way of healthily blowing off steam with humor, as opposed to the genuinely hateful comment of the bystander.

What was their worst fight? "Of course I skewer him

sometimes," Allan said. "I complete thoughts for him." Then he added, "I was for Obama, and once a woman at a party asked me to name one thing he accomplished. I listed several. I enjoyed it—it was like shooting ducks in a pond. But Harry is more difficult because he's so well informed." This was one of the very few moments that Harry had nothing to say in response. Respecting and admiring your adversary in the spirit of (mostly) friendly combat is essential to make this work.

It is noteworthy that neither Harry nor Allan can even remember the topic or the content of their worst fight. That is because the perennial process of fighting is itself what matters, not any individual bout. "We can compartmentalize this," Harry explained. Allan seconded him: "I love a good debate." As hard as it is for painfully embroiled couples to imagine, these two actually relish their back-and-forth. It is intellectually and emotionally alive for them.

The way they handle the often incendiary issue of sharing partisan articles reflects the mutual consideration on which their relationship is built. Allan recalled, "One time I told Harry, 'Look, if I find something that supports my views, would you read it? And of course you send something to me that supports your side, and I'll read it, too." "We do this infrequently," they said in unison—which is one of the reasons their articles are so well received. The tact of this exchange is as impressive as it is rare.

What they have achieved did not happen by itself; there are implicit guidelines, diligently followed. "We have a rule," Allan told me. "We try not to lose our temper with each other; that wouldn't be right. People lose their tempers when they're backed into a corner like a rat."

"Yes," Harry agrees. "It's only politics. I take this seriously, but it doesn't define my life."

"He's quite intelligent," Allan says, "so how can he be a Republican? Maybe he's genetically predisposed."

"And he's a nice guy and we get along, a good friend," Harry retorts. "I check out his good points so I can refute them the next time."

Allan cites a recent example of his friend's astuteness. "When the tax bill was pushed through by the Republicans, Harry made a good point. He said that most people will see a bit more on their paychecks, which would look impressive. Then I saw that *The New York Times* said the same thing. But Harry thought of it first."

For once, and once only, Allan lets Harry have the last word.

※

Being in an intimate mixed political relationship is not for the faint of heart. It requires vigilance, sensitivity, self-control, empathy with distasteful, even disturbingly alien ideas—or at least with the person who harbors them—a certain degree of open-mindedness, and the ability to see core principles beyond differences. Ultimately, in every instance, these couples have discovered that more unites them than divides them emotionally, intellectually, and morally.

Because the contemporary world assumes not only that transpolitical intimacy is impossible but that trying to achieve it is of questionable morality or merit, fewer and fewer people have experienced its unique delights. If you exclude a political opponent on the basis of ideology, you might very well be excluding a soul mate, a precious friendship, a deepening of your perspective on the world. Without ever having this experience it is impossible to comprehend how it stretches you, how it causes you to concentrate on what's fundamental and to avoid knee-jerk assumptions pro or con about the opinions you already hold. I am a more thoughtful, informed, and tolerant liberal because my beloved is a hard-shell conservative, and I have no doubt that all these couples, too, would never exchange their obstreperous partners for anything in the world.

Compartmentalizing, avoidance, volume control—a variety of strategies are employed by couples who put politics in its rightful place in their relationships. That place is different, depending on the personalities involved. The most important factor is that the participants *want* to get along, that they prioritize their relationship above everything else. And they have accepted their radical differences as nonnegotiable, which removes the biggest source of discord.

Here is some of the advice by example that they offer—how they think and how they try to behave—from the front lines:

- They avoid internet-fueled controversy at all costs.
- They always defend each other in public.
- They don't have a TV in the bedroom—even the couple who are both on it.
- Each partner thinks about the impact of their political disagreements on the other.
- They have learned to feel empathy for each other's point of view.
- They show respect for each other's intellect and character even in the face of radical differences of opinion—and they don't just feel it; they actively communicate their appreciation to their partner.
- They employ humor to defuse hostility.
- They know what never to say (e.g., "Trump is a fascist" or "Democrats will destroy the economy"), and they refrain from saying it.
- They ask before giving their partner a partisan article, and they do it rarely. They also read articles their partner gives them.
- They know when and how to stop talking before a discussion escalates dangerously.

7

Three Trump Supporters and the Women Who Love—or Leave—Them

The purpose of this chapter is to challenge the widespread but pernicious assumption that whom you vote for defines your fundamental character, and the character of people you can (or should) love. In fact, political like-mindedness may lull you into complacency, and beguile you into assuming more similarities in fundamental values than actually exist; a case in point is the kind of man who announces that he is a "feminist" but watches pornographic videos while minding his infant. Decency, fidelity, tenderness, generosity, the capacity for intimacy, and other qualities that are prerequisites for a relationship that prospers are actually pretty evenly distributed between most mainstream political parties, and are found even among the apolitical. So are selfishness, arrogance, and meanness of spirit. Despite what the red and blue dating websites pitch, political agreement offers no shortcuts to love.

Just as a partner's ideological similarity is no guarantee of compatibility, political differences—even significant ones—need not inevitably lead to unmanageable discord. Rampant cultural polarization blinds people to this reality. In fact, and fortunately, personality will always trump politics as a predictor of connections that last.

*

Here are three emails I received after Trump's election that convinced me of the need for this book. They all reference an article I wrote on this topic several years ago, and describe a spectrum of relationships between men who support Trump and women who abhor him.

From Nick Mansfield, a Trump supporter

I just read a story that you wrote regarding your relationship with your husband Richard. I have recently entered in a relationship with someone whom I am falling for very quickly. Our situation is similar to yours. She is very, very liberal. I am conservative. This past election I was very much for Donald Trump.

There is one issue that is really bothering her: I have a bumper sticker on the rear window of my car of Trump as that little boy figure peeing on the word "Democrats." If Richard had a similar sticker on the rear window of his car, would you demand that he remove it? If she had a little Hillary doing the same thing to Trump I would chuckle and not ask her to remove it.

We have only been dating for two months, but we have the closeness of a couple that has been together for years. I sincerely don't want to mess up this relationship. What should I do?

From Iris Andrews, a liberal woman

The man with whom I parted ways today sent me an article you wrote in the hopes that I would change my mind about ending our short-lived encounter.

We had only dated for a few weeks, but there were sparks and fire in every sense—intellectually, emotionally, and physically, the minute we met. He seemed to be the person I had always wanted in my life. Then I found out that he voted for the man I feel continues to disgrace this country ever more by the minute. There I am, judging another person for this "egregious" vote, while I expect him to accept my vote as benign to his own convictions—and he does accept my vote and views, without hesitation. Knowing this disparity would eventually erode our foundation, I couldn't continue.

I don't know if I can reverse this opinion of him. It's a very intense lack of respect based solely on politics.

What really struck me after reading what you wrote is that you've persevered throughout your marriage, and continued to love and respect your husband, not despite his views, but to circumnavigate around them.

I don't want to continue my life unable to feel passion, compassion, or empathy for someone simply because they view the needs of their world differently than I do my own. This is the first time I've encountered such a situation and have spent a lot of time thinking about it. Now, more than ever—I'm forty-five—I've come to realize that I need to reconcile this disparity. It is likely to come up again, with similar results, if I cannot see past this very thick line I've drawn in the sand.

From Katie Clarke, a liberal woman

I just read your piece about being in love with someone whose views you hate, and it is quite serendipitous. I am in a relatively new relationship (six months) with someone I've known for ten years. I was reluctant to date because of our differing views, but am now almost forty and have realized I need to be more open. Well, we are being tested this week. We are not even speaking the same language. This morning he texted me that he wept over the removal of Confederate statues while I'm weeping over the hatred I see. I'm trying to get us out of the loop and found your article helpful. I love everything else about him but this is really tough.

When I contacted Katie soon after receiving this, I got the following reply:

> We actually split up just last week, unfortunately. There was a lot more going on there than just this tension. If you'd like to interview me about the conflicts in a relationship that did not work out I can help there!

It was touching, and a little daunting, to inadvertently be anointed the "Dear Sugar" for the politically mismatched, a constituency clearly in need of advice. But it was a task I took seriously, and I knew I had the relevant credentials from my own experience—at least up to a point: My conservative Republican husband, to my great relief, never even considered supporting Trump—let alone putting an obnoxious decal on the car—and in fact abhors the man. But we still take opposing views on every hot-button issue (abortion, assisted suicide, gun control, and global warming, to name just a few). I was struck by what a relief and a delight it was for us to be on the same side, more or less, for the first time in four decades. Nonetheless, had he supported Trump, I feel confident he would have had reasons that were not pernicious, even though I would have vociferously objected to every one of them.

I was relieved to see that I was able without much effort to empathize with both sides in the conflicts these correspondents presented to me—a perk of treating patients from many different emotional worlds for forty-five years, and having more contact than is usual for a liberal like me with the conservative world, an experience I never would have had if I had not married into it. What surprised me is that I generally felt more sympathetic to the Trump supporters than to their liberal girlfriends—not on political grounds but because of the refreshing and surprising liberality of the attitudes of the men involved. In two of the three couples who wrote to me, the person who was acting provocatively was the woman on the left. I could also appreciate what attracted these men to these women, and vice versa. And—with one telling exception—I felt strongly that they were made for each other, except in the voting booth.

"I can get politics elsewhere, but I can't get what we have together anyplace else"

Here is my response to the proud owner of the radioactive decal:

> I think you should remove the offending decal, even if it wouldn't bother you if she had her own version of the same; my rule is civility counts, and why give gratuitous offense? Best of luck with your relationship!

Nick responded as follows:

My girlfriend was elated at your answer. So I will be taking your advice and will remove the offensive sticker (soon). I wish you could observe us when we do discuss politics and critique the way we converse during such a discussion. I find it very disturbing and I don't like the direction the discussions go.

His girlfriend, Linda, replied:

I cannot express enough how delighted I was to read the dialogue between you and my boyfriend on such a heavy and heated topic between the two of us. I very much appreciate your helping us sort through this quagmire. Of course, I was elated to see your response to his question about that famous sticker. Love and Peace!

When we spoke after this exchange, Nick, a fifty-eight-year-old bandleader, was candid and serious, belying all my prejudices about fervent Trump supporters whose cars sported urinating decals. He was funny and frank and clearly astonished at his good luck in having Linda's love—they had been together six months at that point—particularly in middle age and after three failed marriages. I told him how impressed I was that he was willing to remove the offending decal. "You put feelings first, and

that's a good sign in a new relationship," I said. He replied,
"There's nothing more important than consideration—
having that sticker on my car was communicating something she disliked." Clearly, he had already learned
something important from this incident.

Nick told me that he really wanted to be able to talk
about politics with Linda, and was struggling to accept that
he could not, but that what they had was worth sacrific-
ing this for. "I'm the kind of person who loves a spirited
debate without name-calling, but she can't do that," he
said. "She's not even open to a discussion. I hit a certain
nerve and all hell breaks loose, especially about abortion.
It's difficult at times—I'm very passionate about what's
going on in the country, and we can't talk about it." I asked
if he had other outlets where he could air his views. "Yes,
I do, but I find it a little disturbing that I can't express any
opinion at all to her; her responses are very mean-spirited."
I felt that he did have a right to call her on her tone, even
if their ideological differences might well be nonnegotiable to the point that, like Carlos and Nancy, they virtually
had to eliminate political topics from their dialogue. "Have
you ever intervened and changed the subject in these 'discussions'? I asked. "I can't, but I don't feel diminished by
that," he responded, which I took as a sign of healthy self-
esteem. "In that case," I suggested, "the only way to go is
to accept that politics is off-limits between you, so seek areas of agreement. Keep your eyes on the prize."

I wanted to understand what he was contributing—besides his political views and their initial vulgar expression—to the discord that marred their fundamentally solid bond: "You've told me about her liabilities—what are yours?" He laughed. "Where do you want to start? I have an extensive résumé of failed relationships. That's why I'm patient with her—I'm not going to let her getting mad at me about Trump end this relationship; it's a test to see if I'm worthy." Both of them have to work to curb their tempers, conquer their fear of differences, and, most importantly, manage their nervousness about being open to intimacy when it has not worked out well for either of them in the past. Politics is only part of it.

What Nick said next was touching and boded well: "I feel blessed to have someone like her—young, beautiful, successful—I'm so lucky! I hope I'll be able to hold on to her. I'm trying to make it work because she's something special, but I do have to watch what I say." I was impressed that he saw that the connection between them compensated for this lack. "Even though we don't discuss politics, we converse very well together," he told me. "We talk for hours and it feels like minutes, and I'm never bored. I can get politics elsewhere, but I can't get what we have together anyplace else." This was an excellent sign.

Soon afterward I asked Linda, who is a fifty-year-old accountant and women's rights advocate, about her reactions to the infamous decal, and the emotions it provoked.

"The first time I divulged my political beliefs was when I confronted him about the decal and told him that it was patently offensive to me," she said. "Before this happened, politics hadn't come up." She was touched that he had sought my advice about it, and overjoyed that he had followed through on his promise to remove it.

Linda had a painful history with men; Nick had been married three times, but she had had only three previous relationships with men in her life, all of which ended badly. A traumatic past—her father was a bigamist, and her mother did not divorce him for years—had caused Linda to avoid the dangers of love and to focus instead on professional success and community service. She was absolutely thrilled to meet Nick. "I rarely dated," she told me, "but then I joined Match.com and got Nick's profile. It was intriguing; it was magnificent!" Neither had included their political proclivities in their online dating profiles, luckily for them.

She had also never seen the back of his car until one fateful night: "So I'm sitting waiting for him, and he was parked with the rear of his car facing mine, and I saw the sticker of someone urinating on Hillary Clinton. I said to myself, 'How could you be so naïve as not to pick up on this? Political ideology is a direct reflection of someone's core values.'" Linda worried that the decal was more than a vulgar political joke, that it reflected a more general demeaning attitude toward women. She had a sinking feeling that she was about to become a four-time loser.

But she stuck to her guns, despite the risk of losing this intriguing man, and he rang true. "I was adamant about his removing that sticker. I said, 'I can't believe you wouldn't understand that it was offensive to me'—and then he reached out to you. He took off the sticker on July 4—which was fitting, because it was about freedom. I understood that he cared enough and was willing to go the extra mile." Nick's gesture showed her that her feelings mattered more to him than indulging in a bumptious expression of bravado. The freedom to share real love is built in part on self-control.

The way that Nick reacted to her distress assuaged her fears. As she came to appreciate how he treated her, her conviction about what a man's politics—at least *this* man's politics—says about his character changed. "Now I find our differences energizing," she said, "but of course sometimes we have our moments. One of the things I love about him is that he awakens my spirit, as no one has before." No man of any political persuasion had ever showed her the consideration and empathy this rabid Trump supporter lavished on her.

Of course, the removal of the decal did not remove all political discomfort for Linda. "It hasn't been smooth sailing," she admitted. Over time, and with some bumps in the road—like Linda's shock and abhorrence when she read his Facebook posts, which she stopped doing at my suggestion—they reached an understanding that political discussion between them was both disruptive and unneces-sary, and not something they had to share, beyond being mutually respectful of each other's positions. Here again, Nick proved sensitive and open-minded, to Linda's surprise and delight. "Nick said he felt very strongly about his affili-ation, but that I had every right to believe differently, that it wouldn't bother him if we had differences, and that he was open to debating with me. He was even open to the possi-bility of changing his mind if presented with actual concrete evidence that would persuade him to change his current views." He said, "We have to focus on what we have in com-mon, not on politics.'" This demonstrated to her that he was a man who recognized what really mattered in life. "Until I met him, I thought politics was a reflection of core values, but now I realize that's not true," she told me. "The real core value is caring about the other person's feelings."

When political disputes were eliminated, the biggest point of contention became how quickly to intensify their relationship. "He wanted to move full throttle immediately, but I needed much more time," she said.

And, true to form, he gave it to her.

"Only his politics is wrong"

The "sparks and fire" that Iris, a forty-five-year-old fi-nancial analyst, told me she felt when she and Eric, a forty-seven-year-old journalist, first met looked like the start of something big. Eric seemed to be the person she had longed for her entire life—intelligent, expressive, sensitive, warm, intriguing, and passionate. Iris was also touched that he had a tender and playful relationship with his children from a former marriage. She and Eric had many things in common, including years of military service abroad. But her opinion of him changed radically and instantaneously when she found out that he had voted for Trump; he later told me that he was so worried about the negative reactions this piece of information had already provoked from other women he had met online—three had left him because of it—that he had removed it from his profile. In the West Coast city where he lived, none of his many charms could compensate for that single damning fact; it was not a hospitable place for an eligible Trump supporter.

Iris persisted in her outrage at Eric's politics and the assumptions about his character that flowed from them, even though she was fascinated to discover that he was a Wiccan, a religion of white witchcraft and nature worship practiced mostly by New Age women that is rare among right-wingers; it was only one of the ways he did not fit the mold she had in her head. "This was not something I had expected at all," she admitted with confused delight. "He continues to be a cacophony of contradictions, and not in the negative sense."

She reported that her coterie of liberal friends had advised her early on, without meeting Eric, that she should "run in the other direction" based solely on his vote—a decree that she agreed with and summarily acted upon, despite her concern that it might be a touch knee-jerk. I was astonished that she would even consider soliciting such biased advice, let alone take it. Were they jealous, I wondered? Forty-two years earlier, when I met my husband-to-be, it never occurred to me to ask any of my (exclusively) liberal friends what they thought of his politics, and I was considerably younger than Iris at the time. The only criterion that mattered to them was that he treated me better than any of the boyfriends (all liberal) who had preceded him. Later, when my friends met him, they were delighted, if a bit taken aback, by his conservatism. But clearly those were different times, or different people.

Despite Iris's rapport with Eric, her attraction body and soul, she simply could not get over his politics—even though he never thrust them in her face, and accepted her divergent political opinions with no difficulty and with far more liberality than she exhibited toward his. She had ended their relationship shortly after they met on this basis alone, and only started to listen to her second thoughts after she read my article on the topic, which Eric sent to her in the hope of winning her back.

Iris, like the other women involved with Trump supporters who wrote to me, had extensive experience with lousy relationships with men with whom she was in total ideological agreement. Besides, these women all told me, they were middle-aged and saw the logic of expanding their horizons in the search for love, even though until recently they had recoiled from the prospect of ever considering someone from the other party. To them, it had been hard to imagine that a principled conservative—let alone one who voted for Trump—could be as honorable as any liberal.

Iris's and Eric's political differences seemed, despite Eric's unusual and exciting allurements, too big to bridge, even though Iris could not articulate why. She worried that she was being unfair, but she could not help seeing Eric's politics as a deal-breaking defect—not just a difference but a reflection of a pernicious moral code. She told me she feared that, over time, his politics would taint her love. She struggled to get past it, and saw the irrationality of her prejudice given the way he treated her, but her bottom line was that her hatred for Trump meant that Eric, too, had a fatal character flaw because he had supported such a man. In her eyes, he was irreparably tainted. Unlike Linda, and despite her own sobering experiences with politically like-minded men, she couldn't shake this conviction. How could she despise Trump and love a man who had put him in office?

To Iris's credit, she worried about her decision to leave Eric on the basis of a single flaw, even after she had acted on it. She knew that if she did not "learn to see past this very thick line I've drawn in the sand," she risked being alone forever, forgoing any promising possibility on a questionable basis. This is why she was open to reconsidering her decision, as anxious as the prospect made her.

It was a healthy sign that Iris was troubled that her "lack of respect" for Eric, and her summary rejection of him (helped by her friends), was based entirely on the way he had voted. She knew it could not be entirely rational. She asked me how I, a fellow liberal, had managed to coexist amicably with a conservative Republican all these years without constant collisions. I said we had devoted a great deal of thought and feeling to working this out over time, and that it definitely could be done if other things clicked. This kindled in Iris a possibility she had never imagined, or seen an example of, before.

Iris was aware of her dilemma. "He's kind, very, very intelligent, dependable—only his politics is wrong," she said. "I've had boyfriends from the same side of the line as me, and other things didn't work." She knew from bitter experience that similar convictions did not guarantee emotional kinship with, or good treatment from, a man. "I'm living in an echo chamber," she said. "I have some thinking to do. Maybe it's not over yet—there's something drawing me in. Why can't I see this? Why does his politics become such an obstacle? Fear makes me unwilling to take a chance."

A major source of Iris's fear, I believe, was the implacability of her hatred for the man he had voted for, and her worry that she could never forgive him for doing so—that she believed it corrupted his entire character in insidious ways. She might live to regret overlooking an ominous portent of trouble ahead.

Despite her misgivings, she did decide to give the relationship another chance after we discussed it. "I am grateful for the help you provided in our conversation," she wrote to me. "It really opened my eyes to see things in a very different light. We're taking it slow—baby steps. I'm acknowledging my fear, but my excitement, too. We're avoiding the massive subject of how greatly we differ politically with the understanding that learning one another's character is the more important aspect of this relationship."

If this, or any, intimate bond is to work in the long run, the "massive subject" of differences, political and otherwise, recedes into the background, while the similarities and complementarities proliferate over time and become the main focus. Would she be willing to do that?

It occurred to me that she might also fear losing her friends if she stayed with Eric, or being diminished in their estimation, just as Eric was in hers when he revealed his political orientation. And since her political convictions are her moral lodestar, she might also feel adrift if she gave herself to someone outside the world she knew. It was a gamble she had never made before, but one I thought might very well pay off.

Six months later, I got a photograph of the two of them

smiling with their arms around each other. "It's very rare that people get a second chance—it opened my eyes and her eyes," Eric wrote to me. "Wherever the relationship goes, you gave her the ability to realize that it's not going to be that bad. You gave us the option. You made her receptive rather than shutting me out completely."

It remains to be seen if they can have a long-term future together—specifically, if Iris can resolve her prejudices and learn to trust in his love and his character—but it is a risk worth taking.

⚶

I spoke to Eric soon after he and Iris got back together. He was elated, but aware of the ongoing issues their clashing ideologies presented, though she was far more troubled—and provocative—about this than he was. "Your article gave new life to a relationship that had gone down the drain," he said. "We've had amazing times since. But we do have different politics, and she wasn't prepared for that dichotomy. I don't support everything Trump stands for, but that gets lost. And it's not that there aren't things about Hillary or Obama that I liked. I'm actually more of a centrist and more tolerant than she is"—an assessment that I thought was quite an understatement. He is a man who acknowledges other people's prejudices and makes adjustments without feeling outraged at reality; he told me, with irony rather than bitterness, that he had been born in the South, "but I got rid of my southern accent when I realized people automatically deduct ten IQ points if you have one."

This was not the first relationship of his that had foundered over politics, a phenomenon that has become disturbingly widespread recently, just as people rarely used to leave their religious, racial, or class enclaves socially. "My last relationship ended after two and a half years when Trump announced his candidacy," Eric told me. "She was a huge Bernie supporter, but then I became Public Enemy Number One in her life—she couldn't tolerate it. Your article resonated with me because you and your husband are on opposite sides of the fence, and all these years you've been able to make it work. That speaks volumes." This was a goal he passionately believed in and wanted to share with Iris. "I'd been looking for a couple with radical differences about politics as a model to show her. It was important that you were a woman and that your article appeared on a liberal site. I wanted her to see it and thought she could relate to it. She wanted tools to try again, and I didn't know how to scale that wall without an example."

Eric tried his best not to rise to the bait with Iris the second time around, but it was clear that she was still a provocateur, making hostile Trump-related comments at every opportunity, which must have hurt and angered him more than he realized. "I took her to an old golf course to show her the historic buildings," he told me, "and all she could say was that 'golf is a fat, rich white man's sport'"—leaving aside some obvious exceptions (i.e., Lee Trevino, Tiger Woods) to this rule. I wondered whether she was testing him to see if there was a Trump-head hiding beneath his engaging façade, but I also told him that he needed to address her hostility directly and expect her to manage it more maturely, rather than always trying anxiously to placate her and to work around it. Otherwise his anger and frustration would go underground and come out in ways that were as destructive to their bond as hers were.

Despite this tension, they seemed to have the makings of real intimacy founded on mutual appreciation and delight in every other arena. "We have many things to talk about as long as we avoid politics," Eric said, "and I don't need to talk about it. We share so much."

After they got back together, Iris still could not contain herself, and even as they became closer she continued, unprovoked, to attack Eric for his political views. Eric showed more tolerance and forbearance for this behavior than I thought was good for either of them. "She understands and appreciates so much about my life, but she still said, 'You voted for that *monster*!' How do you answer *that*?" he asked. "You don't try," I responded. "You can't condone verbal assault out of fear that she'll leave you. These are not discussions. You have to tell her to stop." I had a troubling sense that politics might be providing an outlet for her unprocessed hostility toward men.

Eric tried repeatedly, and unsuccessfully, to justify himself to Iris when he should not have risen to the bait. His anxiety made him afraid to confront her or to insist that she think before she speak or, better, resist the impulse to speak at all and try to understand what compelled her to lash out. Instead, he kept trying to "draw her into dialogue," a desperate and ineffectual strategy. A person who is bent on insulting you is not willing to have a dialogue, even if the insults are confined to politics.

Nick's willingness to be civil and respect Linda's feelings had saved their relationship, but Iris often seemed stuck in attack mode with Eric. "She told me that one of her friends said she would 'reach across the table and strangle me,'" Eric reported. "She shouldn't have told you that, let alone condoned it," I said. "You can't allow it." I suggested that if she ever repeated such a hateful remark again, he might say, "Then you'll have to protect me." She had to put her partner first, as every couple, politically divergent or not, must learn to do.

Whose side is she on? Hostility like this, even if it is confined to only one topic, can wreck a relationship in the long run. A woman as insightful as Iris owes it to herself to examine her motives. Does she feel that she is a traitor to her side because she fell for a Trump supporter, and can only justify sleeping with the enemy to herself and her friends by demonstrating her opposition in this way? Is she really more fearful than she realizes of an intimacy with any man and using politics as a justification to sabotage their bond?

And yet, because people are complicated, they were often truly happy together, enjoying natural beauty and each other's company. He told me he frequently dreamed about kissing her, and when he recounted these dreams to her, she enthusiastically responded. The Trump-hating was encapsulated; still, it must have made him wary, to say the least.

I did my best to facilitate, but they both have work to do. The course of politically mixed love never does run smooth.

·※·

There are no guarantees that either of these relationships will ultimately work out; after all, couples break up for all sorts of reasons, good and bad, that have nothing to do with how they vote. The lives of each member of these politically mixed couples have already been altered for the better by their knowing each other and loving each other despite huge political differences. Their horizons have been expanded, and they can never ever again automatically assume that everyone on the other side is the enemy. This puts politics in its rightful place. Love really can conquer politics, at least some of the time. Like any other kind of love, it is always a risk.

"He was unable to see me as a person"

Katie Clarke, a thirty-nine-year-old editor, had known Chris Schwartz, a forty-year-old physicist, for a decade when they began to see each other seriously. His right-wing politics always gave her pause, but she "loved everything else about him"—his intellect, his adventurous spirit, his helpfulness, his interest in her life. With age forty in sight, she was willing to take the chance, despite her misgivings.

Katie, who was a committed liberal, really exerted herself to make the relationship work, watching Fox News and reading responsible conservative websites to understand Chris—efforts he never reciprocated, even when she "begged" him to watch one program that was important to her. But as she spent more time with him, she became more alarmed at the extremism of his views—which sounded darker and more strident than Nick's or Eric's—even as his willingness to accept her beliefs as legitimate was nil.

Over eight months, Katie began to notice that Chris's political beliefs were far from the only troubling aspect of his behavior; she had uneasily tolerated his arrogant attitude toward waitstaff in restaurants at first, because "my friend's husband behaves this way, too, and he's a Democrat," but the demerits started piling up. "He was negative about everything," she said. "He felt so wronged in every aspect of his life." When she met his family and they were traveling by subway to a movie, "his cousin suggested another route than he did, and he was so furious that he walked across the platform to get away from us." As a fifteen-year veteran of psychotherapy herself, Katie was dismayed that "he felt he was smarter than every psychotherapist." She also discovered that he was drinking to excess. His politics, which veered disturbingly toward the alt-right, started to seem like the tip of the iceberg.

The breaking point came after the Unite the Right white supremacist rally in Charlottesville, Virginia, in 2017. "When I told him I was devastated that a woman protester was killed by the marchers, he accused me of being sympathetic to the antifa"—a militant far-left protest group. "After I had been defending him to all my liberal friends, he texted me that he 'wept over' the removal of Confederate statues, while I'm weeping over the hatred I see. This was a crisis in our relationship; he was unable to see me as a person. I couldn't get past the human rights issues. I was shaken by this—I thought, 'My boyfriend is a monster.'" Unlike Iris's identical but unfounded accusation of Eric based solely on his vote, Katie's had real justification.

This behavior, and the mindset that underlay it, opened Katie's eyes. "When I first wrote to you I was still trying to make it work, but I started to notice how stuck he was in his positions, how angry, hurt, and sad he was." It was not his emotions but the rigidity and arrogance with which he clung to them that she found ultimately unbearable. "I do believe it's possible with some people to have different politics, but in his case it was all the other stuff; his politics, as he expressed them, was a reflection of other aspects of his personality."

A compelling dream confirmed her misgivings: "I was trying to talk to him, and he wouldn't talk to me. I wanted so badly for us to communicate, but I wasn't able to get him to do it." Without mutual communication, any relationship is doomed. Her unconscious told her the truth, and, luckily, she listened.

Katie's conclusion proved to be justified in a disturbing way: "When I ended it, after eight months, he was shocked, horrible, and vindictive. He felt blindsided and immediately took up again with an ex-girlfriend and told me about it."

Still, she recognized that even with his serious personality flaws, he was not devoid of positive qualities. "He was good to me in many ways," she said. "I missed those things for a while, but I had not a single shred of doubt about ending it. The way he dealt with our political differences showed that he had a perennial chip on his shoulder." She had "no ambivalence, and no regrets whatsoever."

I had the feeling that she would be open to a relationship with a more mature, sane, and healthy man, even if he had voted for Trump.

8

What Is a Core Value?

Jacqueline Winters, a seventy-two-year-old emeritus history professor, was very eager to talk to me about a recent experience of hers involving love and politics. "I hope," she wrote, "that you will find my story interesting even though it rejects your hypothesis that it's possible to build and maintain a relationship when one party supports Trump and the other doesn't."

Clearly, Jacqueline was a woman of ironclad convictions, and she did have quite a tale to tell. It started over fifty years earlier, when she was nineteen and just out of high school, and Daniel was a year younger. She remembers their six-month romance as "sweet and innocent"— they never had sex, she informed me, because she was on the rebound from another relationship and he wanted her to regain her trust in men. "Besides," she said, "I learned that he didn't believe in sex before marriage," a conviction that seemed old-fashioned and in some way appealing to her. When they parted ways—she to go to college, he to Europe to become an artist—she was left with enough fond memories to keep in touch with him periodically in between her two marriages.

Then, after she had been divorced from her second husband for eighteen years, and disappointed in several other "prospective suitors," he contacted her on Facebook. Their subsequent conversations augured well, at least in terms of amorous compatibility—"I had nine orgasms during phone sex," she proudly announced to me—and she invited him to visit her in Florida, where she was spending the winter. "I wasn't looking for another relationship," she said, "but since my recollections of him and us together were so positive—and he felt the same—we decided to see if something new could rise out of the old." He arrived for a three-week stay the day after the 2016 presidential election.

But it was not to be; he had voted for Trump.

They were, naturally, engaged with other things besides politics for the first three days of their reunion, but on the fourth day, when Jacqueline raised the topic of the election, and he told her how he had voted, she was aghast. "He said, 'Can't we just give Trump a chance?'" She was horrified and outraged at the very idea—particularly by his use of "we." "There were other potentially troubling issues—like his mansplaining and his unwillingness to discuss global misogyny," she said. "But 'give Trump a *chance*'? That would have been a deal-breaker for me even if the other issues hadn't arisen."

I asked her to explain her drastic conclusion. "Why? Because Trumpism is more than politics; it's a worldview and a set of beliefs that are antithetical to mine. I don't think you can have a healthy relationship with such a strong clash of so many core values." She was quick to assure me that all her friends felt exactly the same way.

I asked her if she had ever known anyone who agreed with her politically and was not compatible personally, or whether it could be possible for anybody to have legitimate, even if misguided, reasons to support Trump. She replied that she did not think a vote for Trump could ever be legitimate because it was always a demonstration of fatal character flaws and abhorrent values—although she did concede that she would be willing to consider forgiving a Trump supporter if he saw the error of his ways and "changed his mind a year later." Evidently she had never encountered a disagreeable person who agreed with her.

Even world-class passion could not mitigate the revulsion she felt about Daniel's vote; it damned him, and destroyed any chance of a continuing relationship between them, immediately and forever. It poisoned her assessment of his character; she would cut him no slack. "He didn't believe in affirmative action, and he didn't want to talk about religion because he believes in God and I'm an atheist." The list of issues about which they disagreed—and that they therefore could not discuss—was so long that "in the end, we had nothing to talk about at all." The remaining two and a half weeks of their liaison must have been awkward indeed.

"He was an extreme kind of person, so we couldn't have intellectual conversations about anything," she said. Clearly, her definition of such a discussion was one in which the parties had identical opinions. "I needed a meeting of the minds—that's been my life." When she heard herself explaining herself to me, she became concerned about how she was coming across. "I'm afraid you think I'm rigid," she said. She was correct, but I thought that her visitor also seemed rigid and opinionated; personality was a bigger deal-breaker between them than politics.

Complete agreement was Jacqueline's prerequisite for any discussion of current affairs, and without it, all other topics of conversation were also closed off. A search for common ground outside the political realm was inconceivable. It's hard to say whether Daniel's obnoxious qualities really predominated over his fetching ones, or whether once she knew how he had voted she dismissed him altogether, so that nothing he said or did could be acceptable to her. She also did not acknowledge or mention her own judgmental attitude and undisguised contempt as possible obstacles to an exchange of ideas.

The traditional streak in his character that had originally appealed to her was not appealing enough to make her try to work anything out, and compromise was certainly not one of her core values. "For a very short while, I had hoped that, finally, I might be able to find the kind of old-fashioned relationship my parents had, but my hopes were dashed," she told me, letting her guard down for a moment. But she quickly recovered and asserted, "I am now back to where I was before he came back into my life—loving being single and entirely uninterested in having another relationship."

Rekindling a teenage romance at an advanced age after two failed marriages would be problematic even if Jacqueline and her erstwhile love had both been left-leaning Democrats, but she wrote him off without empathy, or any effort at rapprochement, even after he had made the effort and taken the risk to reconnect with her. Mutual accommodation is a prerequisite in any close relationship, especially when you can't hide behind shared politics.

*

Traumatic life experiences taught Diana Kennedy, a thirty-nine-year-old teacher, a very different lesson about the relationship between politics and fundamental values than the conclusion that Jacqueline Winters espoused, even though their ideological convictions were essentially identical, and they held them with equal fervor.

Every one of her father's five siblings, with one exception, is extremely and vocally liberal, and most of them are activists for left-leaning causes. Diana shares what she calls their "passionate interest in politics" and, like them, had always shunned David, her father's youngest brother, who had bucked the family tradition, renounced their (lapsed) Catholic faith to become a fervent Evangelical, moved to the South from the Northwest, where the rest of them lived, and joined the military, which they disdained.

Although David is Diana's godfather, she never felt the slightest kinship with him because of his right-wing views; her father, with whose opinions she closely identified, dismissed his politics as "trogloditic," and Diana assented. She had gotten into several bruising fights online with David over Facebook posts as far back as the second Bush administration, and became even more alienated from him more recently when he began publicly stating sentiments that sounded Trumpian to her. "How can he believe these things?" she wondered. "Religiously and politically I'd never seen eye to eye with him. I didn't really get him. I never felt close to him because he was so conservative; he seemed like a fanatic. I didn't realize then that there were values outside politics."

Diana's horizons first began to broaden in 2011 when she had a miscarriage, which devastated her, and she saw how the people in her world responded, and didn't respond. "I never reached out to David or his wife—but she was one of the only people who contacted me," Diana said. "She communicated for the two of them; she'd been through it five times herself, and I'd never known. They had sensitivity and empathy that I didn't experience from anybody else in my family. The two of them were so thoughtful—the other stuff really wasn't that important. I started to care less about our differences; this was a little turning point in terms of how I thought about them. Politics and religion didn't matter so much. They were kind and they called."

This episode was a chink in Diana's ideological armor. Nonetheless, her conviction that politics was the bedrock of personal values, while shaken, continued to stand, and she still felt appalled by her uncle's conservatism. Even though her eyes were beginning to open, and she gave him and his wife credit for their compassion in her hour of need, David's politics—mostly as expressed in his Facebook posts—continued to infuriate her. "I was really involved with liberalism at that point," she said. "I posted political stuff and so did he. I couldn't hold back from responding to some of the inflammatory statements he made—I wanted to change his mind. I thought that if he just knew the information that I know, I could prove him wrong. I didn't realize that trying to debate would have no impact other than to make him dig in his heels even more. What motivated me was that the policies he and his wife advocated were truly hurting other people—how can they be Christians and believe these things? I felt so strongly about my views, and if he responded negatively I couldn't let it go.

"Right after the 2016 election I did things I later

regretted," Diana confessed. "David's son posted an *SNL* skit skewering liberals. I responded with an ad hominem attack because his son was a Trump supporter, and I was disgusted by this. I didn't know then that his father wasn't for Trump himself, but I knew David's daughter had become much more liberal, so I wrote to David, 'At least your daughter has learned to think critically'—a real low blow, an accusation in the form of a compliment to her. I didn't hear from him for a while. He took the high road, and he was sanctimonious, which made me even madder, because I didn't want to be lectured to. The online community is not good; it makes it easier to say the wrong thing." I was impressed that Diana held herself accountable for her prejudices and online outbursts, as few people on either the right or the left have the self-awareness to do.

Diana's assessment of her uncle's character was evolving. Changes of heart are typically slow in coming, because they contradict deeply held convictions, which spring from identifications with people we love or admire—in this case, with Diana's uncompromisingly liberal father, who continued to repudiate his brother and cling to the siblings who shared his politics, overlooking their character flaws. Changing her attitude required Diana not only to see David's actions in a new light but to give up cherished assumptions that shaped her view of the world and of other people, and to think for herself. Nobody else in her family agreed with her.

Then, six years later, came a series of tragedies and shocking experiences that led Diana to life-changing revelations. These events made David shine brighter—not just because of what he did, but because of what others whom she believed she could rely on failed to do. Diana's grandmother, great-uncle, and father died in quick succession, and, once again, David alone rose to the occasion. Her father's fatal illness was particularly agonizing and prolonged. "David was on it," she said, with deep appreciation. "He lives the furthest away of all my aunts and uncles, and he has six kids, and he's busy. He was there and he was totally dependable—he came and visited and made all the arrangements and helped me deal with everything. He sold my grandmother's house. He made sure to be at my father's bedside when he took his last breath, after everybody else had left. He was there through three different deaths."

As is often the case in family crises, there was bitterness and bickering among the relatives, which David mediated. "Two of my aunts were unkind to their sister, my third aunt," she told me, "but David was sensitive and understanding—much more understanding and helpful than everybody else put together."

"Everybody else" included not only the self-absorbed members of her family but her circle of like-minded friends as well—the people who are supposed to come through for you when your relatives disappoint or abandon you. Her intimate liberal/progressive circle turned out to behave as badly as her kin, if not worse: "I had the same bad experiences with friends that I had with family. I was in a New Age community talking circle for two years. We met every two weeks and discussed deep topics like shame. We started to drift apart because they were huge Bernie supporters; they decided I was not a true believer when I volunteered for Hillary when I was living for a while in a red swing state." Not a single member of this group—many of whom lived close by—called Diana or came to see her when her father died. "I didn't hear from any of them," she told me. "I was shattered—these people thought it was enough to comment on Facebook."

The cumulative effect of these experiences completed the profound change of heart and mind that had begun with David's wife's consoling phone call. "All these things showed me that you should never assume that you know who will be there for you," she said. "People surprise you in disappointing ways and also in good ways. There is a sense of loyalty and decency in my uncle that the rest of the family doesn't seem to have despite their politics." She now knows that people who share one's politics do not necessarily share one's values. "I've become more open to my uncle's viewpoint," Diana said. "It includes valuable traditions, like loyalty."

For the first time in her life, she saw that politics could blind a person to what really mattered, not just be a vehicle to express it. "There are a lot of good qualities if you can see beyond political beliefs. I came to appreciate my conservative uncle's personal values when I compared his behavior to the others who agreed with me." I asked how this revelation had changed her. "I became newly able to recognize compassion, empathy, honor, loyalty, and reliability wherever I found them—I can't put a price on that with people. You can only realize this if you can get *beyond* politics. I used to consider myself lucky that I had a family with one political viewpoint. People have said to me, 'Thank God that none of your family is conservative,' but you must not turn away and ignore humanity when you discover it—I can't paint them as racists or whatever." Showing up, she discovered, is love in action.

Diana did more than acknowledge her change of heart to herself; she told her uncle that she had been blind to his virtues and asked his forgiveness. "In the middle of all this trauma, I initiated a conversation with him. My dad was going downhill, and David and I were down in the basement of my parents' house—we were taking care of things together, and I was so frustrated by the lack of response from the others. I recognized everything he'd been doing and I said, 'Thank you so much. I owe you an apology. I feel ashamed of how I have behaved. I'm sorry I said stupid political things on Facebook—those things really don't matter. You've been so reliable and dependable in all these crises. I really appreciate it.' And he hugged me."

．ﬡ．

Linda, the woman for whom Nick removed the obnoxious
Trump decal from his car window at the beginning of their
relationship, had learned the same things that Diane did
about what constitutes an authentic, lasting fundamental
value, the thing by which to judge another person's worth.
"I always thought politics was a reflection of core values—
but now I realize that's not true," she told me. "The real
core value—the only one that really matters—is caring for
the other person's feelings. Before I met Nick, I defined
myself by my political affiliation, but I have learned from
experience that what each of us contributes to our relationship had nothing to do with our politics. Kindness, respect, willingness to respond to form a deeper bond—those
are the core values."

Diana and Linda had learned from bitter and sweet experience to trust the results of what I call "the Chemotherapy Test." This was a concept I embraced when I
noticed that an intimate friend, with whom I was totally
in sync politically as well as psychologically, failed to
come through for me in any way when I was confined to
a hospital room with acute leukemia for a month, and I
compared her conduct with that of my devout Catholic
neighbor, with whom I agreed about nothing politically
but who could not do enough for me. Of course, my right-
wing husband also came daily, read me Jane Austen by

the hour, and slept on the floor many nights when I was too frightened to be alone. It was he who coined the term, based on my experience and his own cancer treatment twenty-seven years earlier. It is engraved on my heart: "When you're lying in bed with an IV in your vein receiving chemotherapy, you don't ask the political party affiliation of the person standing by your side, faithfully getting you through it."

9

We Love the Things
We Love for
What They Are

Now you have met a panorama of individuals, and of couples—the opinionated and the open-minded, the young and the older, the outspoken and the reticent, the religious and the nonbelieving—on the right and on the left. They have one thing in common: all of them disagree passionately about politics with somebody they love and want to change the way they interact.

They also hope to restore their damaged relationships, which they feel are in jeopardy, and they are willing to take steps to do so. This is good news, because a feeling of helplessness, seeing no way out of the political morass, makes change inconceivable.

What have they learned—for most of them reported that they did learn important things from our explorations of this freighted topic—and what can we learn from them?

Happily, very few people emerged unchanged from our interviews and the thoughts and actions that were inspired by them. They knew themselves better, and had transformative insights, both during and afterward, about what was really going on beneath the surface in their political battles. Then they had revealing and productive conversations with each other—some for the first time—and their understanding of both their own contributions and those of their partner's deepened as a result. These insights opened their eyes and gave them hope, bringing relief and opening new possibilities. They saw their political fights in a new light—as psychologically, rather than ideologically, based. And they knew how to proceed to change them.

Another thing they learned is how much they clung to the relentless hope that they could change the other person's mind if they just worked hard enough, and how large a contribution their desperate, futile effort to accomplish this impossible feat had made to the discord between them.

I was struck by how my subjects were able to hear and make practical use of my observations and advice, even couples whose interactions I was afraid were too deeply entrenched ever to change. But I discovered, to my surprise and delight, that when I asked questions that helped them look within and figure out the psychological origins of their awful perpetual quarrels—since endless repetition of a fight is a symptom of an underlying problem, typically unrelated to politics—they were able to come up with game-changing answers. Seeing their interactions in a different light was often all they needed to figure out what was really going on, a new experience in many cases. Then they were able to think further about their own contributions and about what might be going on underneath, rather than simply blaming their partners or feeling that it was their political differences, rather than their attitudes or personality clashes, that made civil exchanges impossible.

The psychological awakening I witnessed so frequently was both astonishing and encouraging, because it showed that even the most seemingly hopeless fights are not always set in stone. Readers can take courage from this, and emulate the many examples of progress in these pages on their own. Introspection is the key.

In one of the most powerful and heartening illustrations of the power of insight, when I asked Christopher Drake why he persisted in mixing it up with his mother, who constantly attacked and insulted him for his political views, he said he did it to avoid being passive like his father. Hearing himself say this helped him realize that actively refusing to engage with her was actually taking charge of the situation in a way his father never could—a thought that had never occurred to him before. Many people need only to be encouraged to think, and when offered the tools to do so, they do it with great perspicacity.

I was also struck by how amenable my subjects were to changing their obnoxious behavior when given alternatives. Phyllis Halperin, the woman who made her husband, Mark, watch Fox News in the basement, also admitted to thrusting unwanted articles on him on a regular basis. When I told her she had to stop, she replied—to my astonishment—"I can do that." And she did. And it made a huge difference to her husband and to their relationship.

Steve Nelson, the man who had succeeded in alienating most of his family with his online political rants, was afraid that this behavior was about to cost him his beloved sister, Sheila, the last of his relatives to maintain any contact with him. He took to heart my recommendation to tell Sheila—by phone or in person, not online—how much she meant to him, and this restored their bond.

The most important thing—the only essential thing, in fact—in making mixed-political relationships work is the ardent desire to do so; everything follows from this. Change occurs once you are willing to scrutinize your own behavior and its origins, to see yourself through the other's eyes, to listen with as open a mind as possible to your intimate opponent, and to alter your behavior as a result.

Examining your own contribution to these disputes, and the self-knowledge you gain from doing so, is the key to transforming your relationship from contentious to cooperative—even though you still will not, and probably never will, agree on many important political issues. This cannot be avoided; any two people, ideologically aligned or not, always have some basic disagreements because they have different personalities. Fortunately, insight makes empathy possible—and it can be cultivated by anyone who makes the effort. My research demonstrates that when you behave differently, your opponent reacts differently.

Self-analysis is a big, rewarding job with benefits beyond even political peace. Once you decide to do it, you will begin to see connections between past and present—and between politics and everything else—that you never noticed before. Nothing is more fascinating or fruitful to discover about yourself.

Be assured that you can keep your principles intact. Empathy does *not* require identical points of view; as Dylan Marron, one of my podcast guests with a podcast of his own, said, "Empathy is *not* endorsement." It is possible to seek—and to find—spacious common ground outside of politics, because, as we have seen, politics is by no means the only way that fundamental values are expressed. This requires us to recognize that political views are not equivalent to moral foundations; otherwise, it would be impossible for a liberal to believe, for example, that someone who supported gun rights or opposed abortion could be worthy of love and admiration and respect—sometimes more than someone whose political views are aligned with their own.

Love—true love, the lasting kind—is never just looking in the mirror.

How to Be Your Own Politics Doctor

How can you approximate on your own what I did with the couples I interviewed?

Analyze how you fight. Knowing your own contribution jump-starts the process of change. A clear-eyed assessment of your own role is something you can do independently of the other person, and you can start immediately. Begin by making a fearless inventory of your own noxious behavior. And if the description below sounds all too familiar, take heart. You can cure it—or at least modulate it—by recognizing the symptoms.

Is This YOU?

1. You initiate unwanted political "discussions" with hostile comments (e.g., "Did you see that outrageous remark Trump made on Twitter today?").
2. You keep talking about your reactions to the

news, even when your partner makes it clear that he or she wants no part of the discussion by falling silent, walking away, or asking you to stop.

3. You barrage your partner with opinion pieces from your point of view but refuse to read, watch, or listen to anything from the other side.

4. You make it clear that you consider that by voting as he or she did, your partner is personally responsible for the destruction of democracy or the American Way.

5. You rarely discuss politics in a normal tone of voice but yell, bark, or weep instead. You roll your eyes regularly.

6. At the next opportunity, you pick up the fight where you left off, ignoring the other person's feelings or desires.

7. If your partner says something provocative, you never fail to rise to the bait. You excuse yourself by saying, "I can't help it."

8. You are so outraged by your partner's opinions that you cannot imagine any merit or legitimacy whatsoever in them. Conversion is your only goal.

The time to begin your self-inquiry is now, before politics gets even more vicious and divisive. But how do you look beneath the surface to discover the emotional origins of your battles? Below are some thought-provoking questions to ask yourself about the origins of your own emotions and behavior with your beloved political opponent, based on the questions I asked my interview subjects and considered for myself. Ask them with an open mind—and make yourself receptive to the answers even if they show you in an unflattering light or evoke painful past experiences and relationships. Be patient; awareness will dawn on you. It's always a relief.

Realize that just the act of asking these questions will help you find the answers because it reveals the true origins of the political turmoil that is battering your relationship. Focusing on the emotional meanings and possible repetitions of disturbing experiences that made a deep impression on you takes you from the surface to the depths. Identifying the sources of combat is essential for disarmament to succeed; it then becomes clear that your beloved is not your enemy.

I also recommend paying attention to your dreams, which are an unvarnished, and underutilized, source of unconscious self-communication. They show you truths you were not aware of in your waking life—like the dream that Meghan, whose father bullied her relentlessly about her political opinions, had in which he was dead but arose from his coffin to deliver his own eulogy, a humorous but accurate picture of the lengths to which he would go to have the last word.

A general rule to direct your inquiry is to ask yourself what's underneath—how the psychological is manifested in the political. Do not get seduced by the surface conflict, however compelling it may seen. As we have seen from the interviews, this shift of emphasis from the political to the psychological can produce revelations.

Five Basic Self-Inquiry Questions

These questions will help you discover the historical and psychological origins of your political behavior:

1. Does this person's behavior or personality remind me of anyone in my family?
2. Why does arguing with this person make me so furious? Did I ever feel like this earlier in my life, outside the political realm?
3. Do I want my opponent just to listen to my perspective, or is my real agenda changing his or her mind? What does this reproduce from my history?
4. Why do I think that getting through to this person is so urgent?
5. What is it about the way we interact (apart from the political content) that sets me off, and why? If my partner doesn't want to talk about some

topic in the news, or I see that trying to discuss it is going nowhere, why do I persist and insist?

Advice for the Politically Challenged Couple

While you're working on self-awareness and understanding the sources of the problem in your own history, you can also make use of "The Politics Doctor's Ten Proven Ways to Stop a Political Fight Before It Starts" in your very next political discussion; they are synergistic.

What follows is a compendium of advice on how to transform the tone of a politically dysphoric relationship, starting with your own contribution. Behavioral change grows out of self-awareness but can also bring it about, as smiling has been shown to make people actually feel happier. These recommendations are culled from my life experience, my psychotherapy practice, and, especially, what my interview subjects have taught me. Taken to heart, and practiced, they can lead to accord across the aisle, among many other benefits. Just the sincere effort itself will make you feel less angry and more in control, and your partner will notice this. You may discover, as many of my subjects did, that you become closer, more accepting of each other's differences in other areas besides politics, and more appreciative of your relationship than many couples who start out agreeing and never have to make the effort.

Much of what I suggest seems like common sense, but I have discovered in my own life and work that knowing what you ought to do rarely allows you to do it if there are inner obstacles, fantasies, or implicit agendas in the way. Therefore, I believe it is essential both to assume and investigate every possible impediment in your own attitudes, prejudices, and fantasies about the other side. This is critical to undo entrenched patterns of interacting with those who disagree.

The Politics Doctor's Ten Proven Ways to Stop a Political Fight Before It Starts

1. Do not raise your voice.

Your opponent will interpret even a slight increase in volume as shouting. It's a guaranteed way to escalate hostility and makes your opponent automatically shut down and stop listening. Rational discussion will then become impossible.

2. Friends don't let friends drink and discuss politics.

It's hard enough to react well in difficult conversations when you're stone-cold sober, let alone when you've had a few drinks.

Peter and Jake, the gay Trump-supporting couple I interviewed, were in the habit of getting into political arguments about the president's character after they'd had quite a few drinks. This inevitably led to yelling (see tactic #1 above), slammed doors, and, on one occasion, a smashed cell phone. Shortly thereafter they agreed never again to mix alcohol and politics. Learn from their example.

3. *Never* thrust an unsolicited partisan article or link from your side of a contentious issue on your mate, relative, or friend.

The way to share partisan articles with your friend or partner (if you must) is to do it the way Harry and Allan did. Allan wrote a note to Harry saying, "Harry, if I gave you an article expressing my viewpoint on something, would you read it? Of course, I'll read something you send me as well."

And they did it rarely.

A corollary of this rule: speak for yourself; don't quote "expert" outside sources. This pushes the other person away.

4. If the two of you can't talk about it, don't talk about it.

There are lots of people on your side that you can talk to instead of the person with whom you can't have a civil conversation about a hot-button issue. You know what they are. Make conscious avoidance of destructive controversy a joint decision, and don't violate the contract. Part of maturity is recognizing that there are some issues that cannot be discussed between you without misery ensuing.

You can still be true to your beliefs without foisting them on an unwilling audience.

5. Start *no* political conversation with "How can your side possibly think . . . ?"

This is not a conversation starter. It's an indictment. You automatically turn off and infuriate the other person by signaling that you abhor or disdain his or her stance. You cannot have a rational or amicable discussion after delivering an insult.

6. If someone else who agrees with you publicly mocks or insults the political opinions or character of your partner, it is your obligation to defend your partner. This must be mutual.

Not to do so is rightly interpreted as a betrayal.

7. *Do not read* your intimate opponent's political posts on social media.

You know in advance what you'll find there, and you'll be tempted to bring it up (see #5 above). Consider doing this as taboo as reading the other person's diary—even though online comments are public.

8. *Never* conduct a political fight by email or text.

It seems simpler, but it's easier to misinterpret and is offensively impersonal. If you really want to talk something out, call, write a real letter, or arrange to meet in person.

9. Assume decency and goodwill in your opponent, even if you passionately disagree with him or her.

Mutual respect is a prerequisite for civil conversation, and an essential part of love.

10. Accept that political fights are unwinnable.

Realize that you can never, ever change another person's mind about politics or anything else—and stop trying. This mental action instantly restores civility and opens lines of communication between the two of you. It is radically different from explaining your own position with no hidden agenda, which actually works.

It is a universal fantasy that we can change other people—especially people who matter to us—by our powers of persuasion. It is this refusal to accept the limits of our influence over others that makes us feel helpless. The upside of acknowledging this fundamental law, in love and politics, is that once you give up trying to do the impossible, you automatically improve the quality of your dialogue and win the other person's trust. It might even save your relationship.

Media Manners

Partisan media so dominates our political lives now that we need to establish rules on how to manage our exposure and prevent its pernicious effects, if goodwill is to prevail. Contemporary political personalities, especially on cable television and ideological websites, have created a new template for intimate political discourse, and it is a terrible one; any relationship or political discussion modeled on these slugfests is headed for mutually assured destruction. The Hannitys and the Maddows, not our partners, are the real culprits, and we must consciously strive not to emulate them; what is good for ratings is catastrophic for relating. The malignant—and addictive—media environment distorts couples' ability to communicate authentically, and to remain amicable when they disagree. Help your relationship thrive by limiting your exposure.

How *Not* to Argue Like They Do on TV

Follow these guidelines for navigating media and protecting your relationship from invasion by divisive partisan anchors:

1. Remove the television from the bedroom if it currently resides there; if television correspondents John and Margaret can live without one there, so can you. The two of you must create a cordon sanitaire, literally and symbolically, to honor and preserve the sphere of intimacy. Doing so relegates politics to its proper place, always secondary to what matters most.

2. Watch or listen—at least occasionally—to serious, rational voices from the other side, either together or apart; they may be hard to find, but they do exist. Ask your partner for a recommendation—you owe his or her ideas a (nonranting) hearing.

3. Should you choose to watch the news together, turn down your own emotional volume when you turn on the set. Refrain from obnoxious comments about what you see or hear. Never censor what your partner listens to, although you have a right not to listen yourself. That's why headphones were invented.

4. If you ever choose to watch Fox or MSNBC to-gether, resolve to keep your negative opinions to yourself. Do this because the relationship is more important to you than the need to be right. Banish from your mind even an unspoken plan to convert the other person to your point of view about any issue that is being discussed. He or she will know instinctively that this is your goal, and nothing good can come of it.

5. Social media is at least as dangerous to mixed couples as commercial media. Write what you will there, but remember that your mate can read it, so use discretion. *Never unfriend!*

Restoring and Maintaining Civility When You Talk Politics

Now that political discussion with intimates has be-come a blood sport, we desperately need a contemporary manual for these exchanges. The best model I know of is George Washington's *Rules of Civility and Decent Behavior in Company and Conversation*, the guide to conduct, consideration, and sensitivity to other people's feelings that the famously diplomatic first president hand-copied in his youth and modeled throughout his life—a life requiring constant contact with political opponents. Inspired by his example, I offer the following principles:

The Politics Doctor's Rules of Civility for the Politically Ill-Assorted

1. Instead of the ever-popular knock-down, drag-out fight, substitute one of the following approaches to political discussion:

   The horse race: Talking about politics as a sport—who are the players, who's ahead, who's behind.

   Nuts and bolts: Discussing political theories or policy minutiae (which plan will insure more people, will Kim disarm, what does the other person's side believe about X). A good choice for policy wonks.

   The scholarly exchange: Explaining to one another—without ulterior motives—where you stand and why, including your ignorance and your doubts, and any common ground you can find. This became my personal favorite once I realized how interesting and informative it could be to talk this way with a thoughtful member of the opposition.

2. Ask, don't tell. Instead of starting a political discussion armed for bear, try this: "Explain to me why your side is taking this position"—and then listen to the explanation. This immediately lowers the temperature and shifts the emphasis. But it only works if you really want to know—and if your tone is respectful, not accusatory.

3. Never override, dismiss, or denounce your partner's point of view on any issue. Acknowledge your radical disagreements, but do not thrust them in your partner's face.

4. Apply a principle that psychotherapists rely on: never attack the other person's resistance or defenses directly, which only entrenches them. Instead, search sincerely for common ground, try to empathize, and mindfully choose not to speak up when it will lead nowhere.

5. Remember that your partner has legitimate reasons for his or her positions, just as you do. Eschew any attempt to deride, convert, or override him or her. This sets the tone, breeds empathy, and opens the way for true dialogue and mutual respect, even though you passionately disagree. Acknowledge your own principles, but do not try to persuade your opponent.

6. Refrain from interrupting, insulting, or otherwise showing contempt for your opponent's views. None of these either charms or persuades anybody, ever.

7. Speak for yourself. Never quote outside authorities to bolster or justify your point of view—you're not giving a public lecture or writing a scholarly paper in your bedroom or at the dinner table.

8. If someone asks you what your partner thinks about a burning issue, suggest that the person ask your partner directly. Refuse to either apologize for or be sucked into ganging up on those who matter most to you.

9. Remind yourself regularly that your partner is a separate person whose views are no reflection on you. They are an integral part of him or her.

10. Cultivate "the Gift of Silence"—the ability to hold one's tongue that Washington possessed and that impressed everyone who knew him. This takes lots and lots of practice, but it pays off handsomely.

11. Talk *with* each other about how you talk *to* each other. List your hot-button issues, and discuss how you both want to handle them. Every couple has different needs and solutions. My husband and I opted for avoidance tempered

with abstract discussion on our radioactive
topics.

12. George Washington said, "We must take men
as we find them," and the tolerance he expressed
was a cornerstone of American democracy. Make
this your mantra.

13. Differentiate between what you can say to like-
minded friends and to your partner.

14. Contribute privately to any cause you believe in
without making an announcement to your partner, and suggest that your partner do the same.

15. Think about what you love and admire and
cherish about this person despite his or her politics, and tell him or her.

Can (or Should) This Relationship Be Saved?

Sometimes even the best advice and the most sincere efforts to make and keep the peace have their limitations.
How do you decide, after all your efforts, whether your
relationship really can be preserved, improved, or transformed—or whether it is doomed? You can learn to
manage your anger and frustration about political dispar-
ities, but you can't alter the other person's fundamental
character. Some people's personalities, including their
political views and the way they express them, will never

fit with yours, no matter how much you wish it could be otherwise. Many people simply cannot tolerate a mate who disagrees on critical burning issues like gun control, immigration, or abortion; love across the aisle will not work for them. There has to be enough outside the political realm that you don't want to live without for you to endure what you deplore, and other aspects of your temperaments must work well together. This applies to friends as well as partners.

For example, Sandy Kaplan badgers her husband, Dan, daily, but he deals with it by judicious silence. Why does he tolerate her hostility over their political differences? "I admire everything [else] she does," he told me, and—outside of his newly minted Trump support—the feeling is mutual, so their marriage remains intact even though it has been shaken. But Katie Clarke's boyfriend, Chris Schwartz, the alt-right sympathizer, had to go, because she came to realize that his noxious political opinions were integral to his character; he allowed no room for her opposing point of view, did not respect her feelings, and hatefully accused her when she disagreed. Despite his intelligence, her distress and outrage grew over time. She concluded that he had grave emotional handicaps well beyond his ideology—and she knew she was right to leave him by how relieved she was to have him out of her life.

There are also deeply loving relationships in which there is a large discrepancy about the need to discuss politics.

Carlos and Nancy exemplify this. In their case, because there is also so much mutual love, empathy, and admiration, they can both bear a degree of discomfort about the compromises they have to make about what gets discussed and what cannot be. And they have no doubt that this compromise is worth it.

As Robert Frost said, "We love the things we love for what they are." Trying to change them sullies that love.

If you need another remarkable and unlikely example to inspire you, consider the Supreme Court justices Ruth Bader Ginsburg and Antonin Scalia. They agreed on hardly a single controversial case during their shared years on the Court, but they were beloved, intimate friends from the 1980s until his death in 2016. They spent a great deal of time together but never talked politics socially. Their mutual admiration was matched by the antithetical character of their opinions. In *Scalia/Ginsburg,* the comic opera about their relationship, there is a duet that says it all: "We are different/We are one."

Let this be the anthem for all loving politically rivalrous couples.

***

There is one more political odd couple that I want to tell you about. I have insider information on their relationship, and how it has evolved over as long a period as Ginsburg and Scalia's: my husband, Rick Brookhiser, and me.

I'm focusing on one aspect of our union that has meta-morphosed in a way that amazed me, and that I consider a real triumph for both of us: the way we deal with our diametrically opposed, eternally irreconcilable, views on abortion versus right to life. The passionately held convictions that have made this the worst source of potentially sundering discord between us for the forty-two years we've known each other have not changed at all, but the way we handle them now is radically transformed—and in a way I never could have imagined when I first realized how serious and entrenched the divide really was. It became clear to me early on that our positions were so fundamental to what we both held dear that no compromise would ever be possible on this issue no matter how hard we tried. For a long time I despaired of finding a way we could ever mention the topic even in passing in each other's presence.

Rick and I came from different political worlds: mine was virtually exclusively liberal, the dominant ideology at the end of the twentieth century that even my Republican father espoused in his stance on social issues; Rick's was unflinchingly hard-shell conservative, both domestically (his parents were unbendingly right of center) and vocationally. When we met he was senior editor of *National Review*, the leading journal of right-wing opinion, founded by William F. Buckley Jr. The only way we could possibly have found each other was the way we did—in a singing group that sang Renaissance religious music for free on the street corners of New York City. Our love of music united us from the very beginning, and our aesthetic tastes and intellectual interests outside the political realm were remarkably in sync. Our wedding was quite a mixed affair: my mentor, who gave me away, had lost his tenured academic position in the McCarthyite purges, and Rick's publisher, one of Senator McCarthy's most avid enforcers, gave a reading. "Bedfellows make strange politics," quipped a friend. Everyone behaved.

In our political discussions during our first years together, Rick was better behaved than I was. Since he was a professional political writer, he had plenty of opportunities to voice his opinions in print or with his colleagues. But I was used to speaking my mind and could not imagine (at the age of thirty-three) censoring myself radically in my own house, or that there ought to be topics a couple should simply avoid for comity's sake. I have to admit that I uttered something sotto voce that I shouldn't have from time to time, but he didn't respond, and I didn't pursue.

The nadir came in 1989, when I read on the front page of *The New York Times* at the breakfast table about the Supreme Court's *Webster* decision, allowing states to place stringent limitations on access to abortion. I knew immediately that this was the beginning of an all-out effort by conservatives to dismantle *Roe v. Wade,* which to me was one of the most essential foundations of freedom and equality ever enacted. And I lost it. I said, half under my breath but audible all the same, "This is the end. I'm going to have to join a protest march." He uncharacteristically rose to the bait and countered, with grim determination, "If you march, I march."

Fortunately, I knew not to respond to his counterpunch and let the tension escalate into real warfare; this was a fight neither of us could win, with the potential to destroy everything that we had carefully built and that we both cherished, without accomplishing anything. We kept our distance, miserably, for the rest of the day—which we had never done over any other topic, political or otherwise. It was torture. I felt lonely and bereft and frightened, and so did he.

That night, we agreed to disagree forevermore but to hold our tongues, and we officially dropped the subject. We pulled ourselves back from the precipice, and we haven't approached it since. I send contributions to organizations that support my side of the issue and so does he, but we don't stick our views or our actions in each other's face. And I don't feel in any way that I have been unfaithful to my principles or let down my side.

Even after that potential debacle, it took another decade for me to fully accept how yawning our political divide was, despite the fact that we *really did* agree about virtually everything else. Slowly I accepted that I had no chance whatsoever of changing his mind, no matter how compelling my powers of persuasion. How could I show him the error of his ways when he believed in his principles as seriously, as fundamentally, as I did? He never even tried to change mine. The moral high ground is dangerous territory in any marriage, and you claim it at your peril.

Living with someone who profoundly disagrees with you makes you think about what you really believe and why; paradoxically, it actually deepens your principles. I believe—and our life experiences together have proven this true—that my beloved's convictions are only as important as the character in which they are embedded. And my husband's is nonpareil.

Twenty-five years after the *Webster* affair, I read another front-page *Times* headline at the same breakfast table. This time it announced that most of the abortion clinics in Texas were being forced to close, stranding desperate women in need and often without the means to go elsewhere. My reactions in 2014 were exactly the same as in 1989, but I behaved differently: I simply said that it troubled me deeply. My husband said nothing at all. I made an unannounced donation—if he reads this it will be the first time he hears about it—and commiserated privately with people who agree with me.

Since abortion rights are forever in the news, and are guaranteed to stay there, I had another opportunity to react more recently, in May 2018, when Ireland passed its referendum establishing abortion rights at the very time that the United States was chipping away at ours once again. This time I said not one word. However, my husband mentioned the headline to me, as a piece of information that would interest me, without any edge whatsoever. I was impressed with both of us.

But the best was yet to come. When I was revising this chapter, the last in the book, my final opportunity to say what mattered most about love across the aisle, I was trying to decide what to keep and what to discard—a fraught experience no matter how many times you've done it. "This is always the hardest part," I said to Rick, veteran author of thirteen books. I knew he would understand and empathize, and reassure me about my own judgment, as only he could do, because I trusted him unequivocally. "I'd hate to leave anything out that I might later regret not including," I said. "But I know, like Mary McCarthy said, 'You've got to kill your babies.'"†

"Aha!" he said, those aquamarine eyes that had first captivated me forty-two years ago sparkling with a sly smile. "Finally, after all this time, you're pro-life!"

I was astonished to hear him say this. Then it hit me how remarkable it was. The unimaginable had happened: we had actually come to the point where we could share a laugh about the biggest, bitterest chasm between us—a laugh of camaraderie, full of awareness, free of judgment. I was overwhelmed with delight and joy.

Then I kissed him.

---

† This cynical, if realistic, piece of advice to writers is attributed to numerous sources; this is the version I know.

ACKNOWLEDGMENTS

This book is a product of true bipartisan cooperation. I had the most generous help from couples of all political persuasions, who believed in the project and spoke to me frankly, insightfully, and passionately about their struggles to find a way to stop fighting and start talking. Many of them not only gave me interviews, but also appeared as guests on the first season of my eponymous podcast. What they said was a revelation.

The spectacularly capable, creative, and patient staff of Macmillan Podcasts—especially Alyssa Martino, Associate Director, and Alexander Abnos, Senior Producer—continue to teach this baby boomer about this thrilling, intimate new media world. Kathy Doyle, Vice President of Macmillan Podcasts and QDT, offered me sage and enthusiastic advice. Working with colleagues like these is a memorable experience.

Jonathan Haidt graciously tweeted word of this project, which brought me many thoughtful subjects.

This book could never have been written without the enthusiastic and generous help of my good friends at *National Review*, where I first learned about grace across the aisle in the forty-plus years I have loved one of its Senior Editors. E. Garrett Bewkes IV, Publisher of *National Review*, tirelessly recruited intriguing subjects for me; Charles C. W. Cook, Editor of NationalReview.com, let me solicit subjects on the site; and Kathryn Jean Lopez lent her loving support.

My editor, Adam Bellow, made this project his own, and honed it at every turn. His belief in me and enthusiasm for my work are precious to me. Editorial Assistant Kevin Reilly could not have been more helpful.

My husband, Richard Brookhiser, inspired every word—and read them all.

Being married to him has expanded my life and my understanding in ways I could hardly have imagined.

This book is dedicated to Bert and Nina Smiley, dear friends for three decades.

INDEX